Great Houses of Europe

Great Houses of Europe

Edited by Sacheverell Sitwell
Photographs by Edwin Smith

SPRING BOOKS
London · New York · Sydney · Toronto

GREAT HOUSES OF EUROPE
Original edition published 1961
© 1961 by George Weidenfeld and Nicolson Limited, London

This edition published 1970 by
The Hamlyn Publishing Group Limited
London · New York · Sydney · Toronto
Hamlyn House, Feltham, Middlesex, England

Designed by Mark Boxer
Printed in Italy by Arnoldo Mondadori Editore Officine Grafiche
ISBN 0 600 33843 6

Contents

Introduction

CASTEL DEL MONTE

CASTELLO S. GIORGIO, MANTUA

PALAZZO MEDICI, FLORENCE

'THE NOBILITY, this exclusive and exacting class', so runs the opening phrase of a recent book on castles and mansions published in one of the lands behind the Iron Curtain, and it then goes on to illustrate and describe more than eighty houses in the thirteen provinces of the country in question which was part of the former Hapsburg Empire. It is a grudging tribute, as would be that of critics of a like mind, haters of both Church and State in the old meaning of those terms, who must yet acknowledge Chartres and Versailles as the most splendid and enduring monuments of France.

But it would be wrong to allow credit, or lay blame, according to point of view, only upon the class of persons indicated in such deprecating words. For, over and over again, their ranks were swelled and their blood renewed and vitalized by families of middle class or much humbler origin. Rather it could be said that the Great Houses represent the aspirations, if not the achievement, of all classes of the community. As such, they are the fine flower of western civilization, and of more tangible reward than our churches with their constant reminder of the tomb.

In the world of antiquity the Roman villa offered some points of resemblance to our country-houses. The mysterious Piazza Armerina in the middle of Sicily, on an imperial scale of grandeur, with mosaics of hunting scenes and of girl athletes or acrobats – a mystery because of its pagan feeling in a mostly Christian world and the uncertain identity of its builder – was certainly a country house and had amenities denied to the dwellers in our castles and mansions of ten centuries later in time. And Diocletian's palace at Split, in Dalmatia, which still encloses the old town within the periphery of its walls, was as surely and certainly a country or, rather, a marine palace.

Perhaps in the ancient world one would have most liked to see the palaces of the Byzantine emperors at Istanbul, occupying the present site of the Old Seraglio upon the Golden Horn, and forming the highest achievement of the arts of decoration in the west, and probably in all human history. Just as, in the mosaics of San Vitale at Ravenna, it is the group of the Emperor Justinian and his courtiers and that of the Empress Theodora with her eunuchs and ladies-in-waiting that hold our attention, so, in the Imperial palaces of Istanbul it would be the secular subjects in mosaic, more than the religious, that would be our magnet. It is a sensation just to read, or be told, of these. The Chalce or great porch of the palace, where were portrayed Justinian and Theodora, the conquered towns of Italy, Libya and Spain, Belisarius bringing the loot and the prisoners to the feet of the Basileus, and a banquet and festival in celebration of triumphs over the Goths and Vandals, all in mosaic; the Camilas, a hall that has a roof flecked with gold, and mosaics with scenes of harvesting and reaping; or the halls added by Basil the Macedonian in the ninth century with mosaics of his warlike exploits, his Empress Eudoxia and their children; and a summer retreat open to the Bosphorus with walls adorned with the hunting of lions in mosaic, trees and flowers and animals and scenes of fruit-gathering. What would we not give to be allowed a glimpse of these!

Talk of Byzantine mosaics leads on to tapestry, which is a Gothic art, and already we are in the Middle Ages. Castel del Monte, the octagonal castle of Frederick II, 'Stupor Mundi' in Apulia, built in about 1240, is this a hunting-castle or a country palace? For Frederick II was half-oriental in mind and habit. Are we to relate it to the hunting-castles of the Ommayad Caliphs that he may have seen in the deserts near Damascus or Jerusalem, and that had Salome-like paintings of nude dancers on the walls? Frederick II who settled his Saracen bodyguard at Lucera, and whose marble dining-table now serves as high altar in the Cathedral there.

We move up the Adriatic coast of Italy to find ourselves at the Ducal Palace of Urbino, the first of our Great Houses. This is a beginning to the book which imposed itself, for it would be difficult to exaggerate the exquisite detail of the doorways and chimney-pieces, and the almost therapeutic property of its delicate proportion. Here lived Duke Federigo of the broken nose and his Duchess Battista Sforza, known to us by their double portrait by Piero della Francesca in the Uffizi; and we may think of them, as of the allegorical paintings on the back, processing through the landscape on chariots drawn by unicorns to this early Renaissance palace of all palaces.

After Urbino, the choice is more difficult. The Great Houses proliferate and spread to nearly every country in Europe. By no possibility could all of them be included; the subject has had to be dealt with by selection, and the course taken by the writer of this Introduction is to steer his way among the material chosen, while supplementing it, and where possible illustrating his text, with houses not mentioned elsewhere in the body of the book. For instance, the Palazzo Medici at Florence is of almost the exact date of the Ducal Palace at Urbino, and behind its rusticated exterior of golden stone by Michelozzo, the Magi are on their journey through the Tuscan landscape of spring flowers and cypresses and stone pines in the frescoed chapel by Benozzo Gozzoli. What a beautiful world, with the paintings by Beato Angelico in San Marco only just down the street. We can only illustrate, and just mention, the Palazzo Strozzi, like a huge golden chest or coffer of the burgeoning Florentine Renaissance; or the country palaces by Rossellino at Pienza, built to the command of Pius II (Aeneas Sylvius Piccolomini) who appears in one of Pinturicchio's frescoes in the

PALAZZO STROZZI, FLORENCE

PALAZZO PICCOLOMINI, PIENZA

REGGIA GONZAGA, MANTUA

CHENONCEAUX

PALACIO DEL INFANTADO, GUADALAJARA

PENA PALACE, CINTRA, PORTUGAL

VILLA BADOER, BY PALLADIO

ISOLOTTO FOUNTAIN, BOBOLI

Piccolomini Library at Siena as improbable envoy from the Council of Basle to King James I of Scotland.

Together with these great names of Italy and the Renaissance comes Mantua, where the Reggia or Corte Reale of the Gonzaga with its damaged frescoed paintings of the family by Mantegna, its rooms frescoed by Giulio Romano (the only painter whom Shakespeare mentions) with the Wars of Troy, and its dwarf's apartments, make a sum total of the most beautiful of Italian palaces after that of Urbino. The immense size of it perhaps precludes entire enjoyment; and where the Gonzagas are but invoked there must be room for the name of d'Este, of inseparable association with the arts and with poetry in the persons of Ariosto and of Tasso. But of their palaces little is left except the frescoed room by Cossa in the Palazzo Schifanoia.

THE fever has now spread to France, and the transition from Gothic to Renaissance is shown in the castles of Châteaudun and Chambord. But it is the Gallic Renaissance; just how French it was is exemplified when we think of Leonardo da Vinci spending the last two years of his life, and dying, at Amboise. The chapel there has a stag with a cross growing between its horns over the doorway, like an echo of French hunting music down the rides of the royal forest, and is in florid Gothic. Or, in order to know that this is France, and not Italy, we have only to look at Titian's portrait of François I in the Louvre, remembering that it is this monarch and *galant homme* whom we English accused of tripping up our King Henry VIII when they wrestled together at the Field of the Cloth of Gold, and that is François Premier who built Chambord.

We can follow this French king whose spirit inhabits the châteaux of the Loire – his salamanders are carved on the stairs at Blois, and it could be said that he shares Chenonceaux with a shade surely congenial to him, that of Diane de Poitiers, mistress of his son Henri II – from France to Spain. For having been defeated and taken prisoner by the armies of the Hapsburg Charles V at the battle of Pavia, some of his captivity was spent in gilded ease under the Mudéjar ceilings at Guadalajara. Here the Duque del Infantado entertained him; and from Moorish windows high above the portal, which has for crown a huge armorial shield with satyrs for supporters, he looked down on the tournament held in his honour. The patio of this, perhaps the most strange and exotic of Spanish palaces, has carved lions with heads like hedgehogs over its arcades; and in the interior are chimney-pieces which the French king greatly admired, and superb inlaid and gilded *artesonado* ceilings, the world of Moorish craftsmen. They are, or were, the finest of their kind in Spain; for the Infantado Palace at Guadalajara was badly damaged in the Civil War. In contrast to this, the Casa de Pilatos at Seville has survived uninjured, and is a most perfect specimen of the Muslim inspired houses that are to be found from Marrakesh to Meshed. Nevertheless, it has the distinct accent of Spain that we find in Las Duenas, the palace of the Dukes of Alba, and in the courts or cloisters of orange trees in the mosque cathedrals of Cordova and Seville.

It is time to return to Italy where we can move from Giulio Romano's giants and horses and banquets of the gods at Mantua, in the little Palazzo del Te, to Villa Maser, Villa Lante, Caprarola, Villa d'Este, four master-works of the Italian genius, and each and all of them profound and poetical almost beyond description. Villa Maser, built for two brothers of the Barbaro family, is unique as being planned by Palladio, having stucco sculptures by Vittoria and painted rooms by Veronese, a combination or triple concerto of talents the like of which will not occur again. In the result all is perfect proportion and harmony, as we might say of some masterpiece of music that the acoustics are perfect, the instruments superb, and the performance sublime. Villa Maser is a summer *villeggiatura*, but of what patrician imagining and poetic fancy! The instinct of the writer would put Villa Lante into the same paragraph as Villa Maser, though here the twin pavilions have little emphasis put upon them. All the interest is in the Quadrato or square garden with its parterre, and in the fountain of the four Moors (but they resemble classical athletes) in the middle. The same incredulous wonder comes over one as at the famous 'Moss Garden' at Kyoto. Can it be that those box-hedges, this green embroidery, has kept its pattern since the middle of the sixteenth century? The fountain may or may not be by Giovanni da Bologna and the Villa and garden by Vignola. It matters no more than whether the 'Moss Garden' is really by a Zen priest of the fourteenth century; or than the name of the Arab who designed the garden of the Generalife at Granada. It is enough that each in its kind is a perfect work of art. To compare with the fountain of the Quadrato we could suggest the Isolotto of the Boboli Garden where a cypress avenue leads to a stone island planted with flowers, lemon trees in terracotta pots along its parapet, and above those a statue of Oceanus by Giovanni da Bologna; or for comparison with the parterre of the Quadrato, those of Villa Gamberaia, outside Florence, and the view down over Tuscany beyond the green embroidery. But that would be before we climb between the pavilions of Villa Lante to the pagan wood beyond, its faunal shades of ilex, and the long musical descent of the waters chiming, and all but speaking, in their beds of stone. The Villa Lante is surely the most beautiful of Italian gardens.

At Villa d'Este, the garden, or rather the fountains, are more important than the house. The fountains, and the cypresses, and that huge portico with a view over the Roman Campagna leading down, down to the fountains. Villa d'Este and its cypresses, and that wonderful portico, were an inspiration to Fragonard; while the pyrotechnic display of the water with their jets rising to different heights, which he heard during the many summers that he lived there, inspired Liszt, and little wonder. At Caprarola, the accent is reversed and falls more on the house than on the garden. This is the most splendid of Italian country places – Caserta alone excepted – and its vast shape towers high above the village and the little white church to the left across the valley. It is a sensation to look up at it from the airy terrace in

VILLA GAMBERAIA

CEILING OF CHAPEL, CHATEAU D'ANET

HEIDELBERG CASTLE

CHATEAU D'O

BOLSOVER CASTLE

KNOLE

CHATEAU DE BALLEROY

CHATEAU DE SASSY

front of it. In the interior the circular stair of paired columns gives proof of Vignola's mathematical or geometric genius which we are to admire in his other mood of poetic imagination in the garden. Up the stair are twelve rooms frescoed by the brothers Zuccaro with paintings that play the part of tapestries. There are fountains of coloured stucco in one or two of the rooms that prepare us for the wonders of the garden; for the moss-grown Atlantes and river-gods, and on the highest terrace of Caprarola (with the two goat-syllables in its name!) the caryatid statues or garden-terms of fauns and faunesses with baskets of grapes upon their heads to crown their goat-locks; single figures, mostly, but in the corners of the terrace they are in pairs and talking together, in dumb language or by signs, as they look down through the ilexes and on to the plain.

After Caprarola – and the Villa Maser, Villa Lante, Villa d'Este – we come to Hardwick Hall, and I can only say to foreign readers who have not seen it that this is a considered opinion and not only the boast of an Englishman: it is, I think, as a building, and in its contents, as beautiful as any of these masterpieces of the Italians. We shall not again in the course of this survey of the Great Houses of Europe come across any structure more beautiful, inside and out, or more varied and beautiful in its contents. A building of the northern Renaissance, not without influence of the Perpendicular, that style unique to England in its huge areas of window and fretted roof-line. The Long Gallery which, when the writer was a child, had four or five thicknesses of tapestry hung one over the other upon its walls, and pictures hung over the tapestries, is peculiarly English, too, and so is the portrait of Queen Elizabeth I in her astonishing farthingale and gown embroidered with snakes and birds and sea-horses. The Great Chamber which has the frieze of hunting scenes in coloured plaster has been apostrophized by the writer as 'the most beautiful room in Europe', and he has seen nothing since to make him alter his opinion. Marvellous, too, are the state beds 'hanging in costly golden tatters', when Horace Walpole saw them, but now mended; while the tapestries, and above all the needlework, are unrivalled. Foreign visitors to Hardwick should not neglect the opportunity of seeing Bolsover Castle, which is but six miles away, and the most romantic and imposing ruin in England with its empty and haunted keep, the riding-school, and the great roofless halls built for the entertainment of Charles I and his court when Ben Jonson's masque of *Love's Welcome* was performed in 1634 with dresses and scenery by Inigo Jones, but burned out soon afterwards.

Hardwick is of the Renaissance, yet mediaeval. Wilton is the first full Renaissance house in England, of the school of Inigo Jones who took Palladio for his model. It is, therefore, the cynosure of our Palladians of a later generation, and the house of houses in which to see paintings by Vandyck. The Double Cube Room, more probably by Webb, Inigo Jones' pupil, is a wonderful English-Venetian triumph of proportion; the huge Vandyck family group covering one wall is an epitome of the cavalier age, while the supporting gilt furniture by William Kent, the Palladian of a century later, is to Inigo Jones what Tiepolo was to Veronese, the total effect being of a Venetian magnificence superior to anything in the Doge's Palace. To that later generation, too, belongs the Palladian bridge in the pleasure grounds at Wilton; 'Venetian' in intent and origin, but as English as the Horse Guards at Whitehall or the Tower of London. But neither Hardwick nor Wilton must be recalled without mention of Knole, the house of the Sackvilles, where the state beds and furniture of the time of our Stuart kings is as wonderful and unspoiled as anything in England.

Hôtel Lambert on the Île St Louis is of the same epoch, Louis XIII, and must be the finest house in Paris. The Galerie d'Hercule, a huge golden saloon on the first floor with paintings by Le Brun, has but the Galerie Dorée of the Banque de France to compare with it in the French capital, and that is in the full flower of the Louis XIV style. The earlier of the two is the more beautiful, while Chopin having played in it gives it a halo of another kind. That we are now in the *grande époque*, and that this means harder lines and a more heartless finish to detail, is apparent at Vaux-le Vicomte, built just before Versailles. It is the age of Le Nôtre, and we are far from Villa Lante and Villa Maser. Canal and glacis are on the scale of fortifications, and the young avenues are long green tunnels open to the skies, but they lack the soul of Caprarola and the poetry of the Italian garden. We miss the silver furniture of the Galerie des Glaces, and the liveries and uniforms and periwigs that would bring the gilded rooms to life; while admiring as examples of Roman magnificence the Orangeries with its great stairs and the Grande Pièce d'Eau des Suisses. Most of all one would wish to have seen the twelve pavilions of Marly; but there is still another garden, that of Beloeil in Belgium, home of the de Lignes, that gives us the full splendour of the Augustan age.

BELOEIL

CA' REZZONICO

A s the style loosens, there is Isola Bella, afloat like Armida's galleon, with terraces for decks, long despised, but musically, melodiously Italian, with the *bel canto* of its camellias and obelisks, its fountains and lemon-trees and pebble-mosaic pavements. Isola Bella is contemporary with the Venetian palaces by Longhena, architect of Santa Maria della Salute, and alike in the sea-dome and whorled shells for buttresses of the Salute, and in the water-façades of his Palazzi, Pesaro and Rezzonico, with their plumed helms for keystones and rusticated, weed-encrusted walls, we have another water-architecture, to rise from and be reflected in the Grand Canal of Venice. Perhaps this is the moment, too, in which to invoke the painted ceilings of Tiepolo; the clouds and white horses of a room in the Palazzo Rezzonico; and at the Palazzo Labia, the disembarking of the blonde Cleopatra – a gondolier's daughter? – from the galleon, and her banquet in fresco among turban'd attendants on the opposite wall. We can follow Tiepolo from his native Venice to the *terra firma*; to the glorification of the Pisani at Strà; to his beautiful walls and ceilings at Villa Valmarana, above Vicenza; to another and fine ceiling at Verona (Palazzo Canossa); and to a little known but

TIEPOLO FRESCO, PALAZZO PISANI, STRÀ

THE ROTONDA, VICENZA

13

HAMPTON COURT

CASTLE HOWARD

RIDING SCHOOL, VIENNA

MAURITSHUIS, THE HAGUE

glorious exercise of his genius as a decorative painter in the Palazzo Clerici at Milan; not forgetting his prodigious fresco of Olympus and the four Continents on the stair at Würzburg, and his *Marriage of Barbarossa* in the *Kaisersaal*; or the last prodigy of his talents on the ceiling of the throne-room in the Royal Palace at Madrid. And to have done with Italian painted walls and ceilings in this same paragraph, let us remind ourselves that, other that Tiepolo, the finest examples are probably those by Pietro da Cortona in the Palazzo Barberini in Rome, and his paintings from the *Aeneid* in the Palazzo Pamphili in the Piazza Narovia of the same city; to end with Luca Giordano painting the Medici as gods of light among the gods of Olympus, in the Palazzo Medici at Florence.

So much for frescoes. In the meantime it could be said that the main currents of influence flowed to most of Europe from Versailles, but inspiration to British architects came from Vicenza. This was a delayed current, it is true, though of a timeless classicism to which others than Englishmen might find it difficult to assign the date. But this does not apply to Sir Christopher Wren, a mathematical genius, a *virtuoso* in the old sense of the term, turned architect, whose Hampton Court Palace is of the red brick Dutch architecture *in excelsis* with touches of Versailles, albeit in a learned Oxford accent. In the person of Sir John Vanbrugh we have a phenomenon of another kind, a fashionable Restoration playwright transforming into one of the most prodigiously gifted and original geniuses of any age. His Blenheim Palace is incomparable in scale; but our foreign readers would be well advised to visit Castle Howard in Yorkshire. Horace Walpole said of it: 'Nobody had informed me that I should at one view see a palace, a town, a fortified city, temples on high places, woods worthy each of being a metropolis of the Druids, the noblest lawn in the world fenced by half a horizon, and a mausoleum that would tempt one to be buried alive; in short. I have seen gigantic palaces before, but never a sublime one.' His words are no more than true of Castle Howard.

F ISCHER von Erlach came to London. So far as I know, Vanbrugh never went to Vienna; but it is perhaps not fanciful to see some slight traces of his influence on von Erlach. The Palais Schwarzenberg was worked on by both von Erlach and Lukas von Hildebrandt; though the latter alone worked at the Belvedere built for Prince Eugene of Savoy; at the Kinsky Palace; and both architects together at the Winter Palace of Prince Eugene with its splendid staircase-hall and statues of Atlantes. The Baroque monasteries in Austria with their great stairs, as at St Florian and Göttweig, their libraries and Kaisersaals and state apartments, are but little different from country mansions. The most magnificent of all houses of Central Europe, the peer of Vaux-le-Vicomte and of Blenheim, is Pommersfelden, its superb stair closely matched, as we have hinted, by the staircase at Klosten Ebrach, a Cistercian abbey only a few miles away. Probably Johann Dientzenhofer had a hand in both of them; and at the latter J. B. Neumann, architect of the palace at Würzburg, was involved. As Baroque turns into Rococo, inspiration becomes refined and subtilized into such wonders as the apricot, and pale blue and silver rooms, of the Amalienburg, outside Munich, by the Court dwarf, Count Cuvilliés, only matched by the golden delicacies of the Reiche Zimmer of the Residenz and the (now restored) Residenz-Theater from the same hand. Such filigree intricacies and prodigies of grace and balance are on a par with achievements of the Saffarid Persians and the Andalusian Moors, though they are equalled by the interiors of many other Rococo churches and chapels in Bavaria.

HUYS TEN BOSCH, HOLLAND

Three 'pleasure domes', which it is a delight to take together, are Queluz in Portugal, Drottningholm in Sweden, and Stupinigi outside Turin. The first of them should be seen through the eyes of 'Caliph' Beckford who, writing of it forty years later, describes the world of his youthful memories, the huge hooped skirts of the Court ladies, the dwarfs, and the poets spouting impromptu verses. He tells of the Italian *castrati* warbling in the Royal chapel, and of 'the oboe and flute players posted at a distance in a thicket of orange and bay tree', playing 'the soft *modinhas* of Brazil'. At Drottningholm it is the Kina Slott that enchants and is perhaps more capriciously fanciful than any of the Ming pavilions, reminding one, though that is not *chinoiserie*, of the Eremitage at Bayreuth. Stupinigi, the masterpiece of Filippo Juvara, with the stag on top of its cupola, in the hunting castle 'where the Sleeping Princess still slumbers, unwoken yet'. Juvara, a great theatrical designer, has here made permanent the old Italian theatre scenery of the Bibienas. There is no comparison to Stupinigi, unless it be another of her palaces, Clausholm, lost in the high woods of Jutland, with snow-white plaster ceilings in delayed Louis XIV style by stuccadors from the Ticino in some fifteen of its rooms, a castle of strange interest as the residence of the 'conscience' Queen abducted by King Frederik IV, as Absolute King, while his legal wife was still living and married to him.

CLAUSHOLM, JUTLAND

Sans Souci, and the other palaces at Potsdam, are the best setting for the rococo of Louis XV, strange bibelots for a Prussian martinet. And if there are not many French houses of the date with all their treasures intact, there are the inexhaustible riches of French furniture which, collectively, form one of the highest fantasies and ingenuities of human hands, a not inconsiderable proportion of the craftsmen being in fact Germans at work in the French manner in the capital of France. The Place Stanislas at Nancy will remain in the minds of all who have seen it, together with the theatre at Versailles, as epitomizing the French style. Louis XV was indeed, under Madame de Pompadour's influence, as much a builder as Louis XIV, but his numerous small châteaux, with their gardens still in the old French formal style, are all swept away, and only the Petit Trianon is left, and that, curiously, is forerunner of the Louis XVI style. The small intimate rooms of Louis XV are of the new age, and it is very typical of this monarch that he should be put to bed nightly with elaborate formality in the state bedroom of his great-grandfather at Versailles, and then repair to other and smaller rooms upstairs. Could we but see

COLONNADE, POTSDAM

KASTEEL MIDDACHTEN, HOLLAND

15

KEDLESTON, THE GREAT HALL

HOLKHAM, THE MARBLE HALL

MOUNT VERNON, VIRGINIA

MONTICELLO CHARLOTTESVILLE, VIRGINIA

the art treasures of the Pompadour we would have the complete picture of the age.

A little prior to this period the mood of England was Palladian, and William Kent its chief practitioner. Lord Burlington is to be associated with this Palladian movement, showing the conservative feeling of that 'exclusive and exacting class' of which he was a member. Chiswick House, lately restored, and the work of Burlington and Kent together, is the most accessible of these Palladian essays; while Mereworth Castle, another of them, is by Colin Campbell, reproducing in the green meadows of England what was native to the Vicenza hills. In order to know Kent at his best it is necessary to go to Norfolk. Holkham must be seen, its great hall of fluted columns 'enriched with purple and white variegated alabaster', and his superb furniture in 'Venetian' style at Houghton. His stair and the coffered saloon at 44 Berkeley Square, London, should be noted; as, also, his landscape garden, the 'Daphne in little' of Walpole, at Rousham, near Oxford; and the Worcester Lodge at Badmington. Only then can his talent, but little known outside England, be appreciated.

ADAM is to be seen near London. Syon House; its ante-room with verde antique columns from the Tiber; long gallery in Italian Renaissance manner with little closets or boudoirs at each end; and the splendour of its doors and door-cases: all these are unsurpassed in design and workmanship by anything in Europe. His 'filigraine ceilings' are to be admired in spider-web delicacy at 20 Portman Square; and at 20 St James Square, splendidly restored, is a house by Adam which he designed *in toto* down to the sedan chair, the ink-stand and the door-knocker. Further afield, at Kedleston, in Derbyshire, is his hall with twenty fluted columns of Derbyshire alabaster, and a pair of grates of burnished brass and steel, with fenders and fire-irons, upon which he lavished the utmost refinements of his skill. James Wyatt, an architect with as much talent but wayless and haphazard in its application, should be seen at Heveningham Hall in Suffolk. The hall with yellow scagliola pillars, double mahogany dining-room door, most sumptuous of its kind, candelabra in the form of rostral columns, and dining-room furniture, are the measure of his originality before he turned to the sham Gothick. Castle Coole, in Northern Ireland, is another of Wyatt's houses, more seriously classical in manner. This style can be followed to Mount Vernon and Monticello, and the pillared porticoes of Virginia and the two Carolinas.

'Capability Brown' and Humphrey Repton, landscape gardeners, were creating the 'English' park and garden. The former is to be admired in the hanging woods and lake of Blenheim Palace. Badmington with its twelve-mile belt or verge of trees; and the deer parks of Longleat, Petworth, Arundel, with their groves and stands of timber are unique to England. In Ireland, where labour was cheaper, the parks are almost artificial landscapes and could be set beside the hunting parks of the Chinese Emperors. Powerscourt may he the most beautiful of these, but there are many others. Russborough, in County Wicklow, is a typical Irish country-house: Palladian outside, with rich stucco-work within, probably by Italian craftsmen. But the native Irish school of plasterers is to be admired in Dublin houses, often become slums, close to Gandon's Custom House, in the city where all lovers of architecture should see the Marino, a little classical casino by Sir William Chambers at Clontarf, just outside the town, a Lilliputian masterpiece on a par with the Petit Trianon.

There are curiosities in England that we do not expect to find there, such as the *chinoiserie* of Claydon, more unexpected that Horace Walpole's Strawberry Hill, or the sham Gothick of Arbury. But we must go back to the mainland of Europe for a last survey which takes us to such houses as Eisenstadt, the country palace of the Esterhazy, on the Austrian side of the frontier with Hungary, with its late classical room, 'English' park, and memories of Haydn. There are other mansions of the Hungarian magnates in the same style; and the castles of the Bohemian nobles, such as Krummau, rechristened Cesky Krumlov, where the Grenadiers of Prince Schwarzenberg were still on guard in 1932, and the masquerade hall is still frescoed with carnival figures looking down from boxes, and harlequins rub shoulders with moustachio'd Hussars. This hypothetical tour could extend into Poland, to castles such as Lancut of the Potockis, or Lazienki with its garden theatre. And further still to Russia, where we are able to illustrate the Youssoupoff Palace in Leningrad, though its former owner assured the writer of our article that he had two still finer houses. It can be no more than an enumeration of names to mention Rastrelli; or the external colour-schemes of the Leningrad palaces, – yellow, or lilac, or salmon, or rich blue; or the Winter Palace which was originally pistachio green, with white pillars and gold capitals; or the Palais Michel in Russian Empire style by Rossi.

We return by way of houses in Ghent or Amsterdam to find Nash at work in England, who should be seen at his best at Caledon in Northern Ireland. His terraces in Regent's Park are matched by the marine squares of Brighton and the parades of Cheltenham. To end with Penrhyn Castle in Norman style with four-poster beds and doorcases of slate, and with the domes and chandeliers of Brighton Pavilion. That exquisite workmanship was still in practice is proved by the Haga Slott outside Stockholm in Pompeian style, built for the playwright King Gustavus II, and by the Casita del Labrador at Aranjuez, an over-exquisite setting for the Goya King and Queen of Spain. The *cottage orné* of thatched roof and honeysuckle, where lived Giselle in the old ballet, is to be seen at Liselund in Denmark, or in the green demesne of Cahir in Tipperary. But the writer is informed that our photographer, who has travelled all over Europe taking pictures of all but two of the Great Houses, is of opinion that Villa Lante is the most beautiful of them all. I would agree with him, and put Hardwick second.

Sacheverell Sitwell

KRUMMAU CASTLE, CZECHOSLOVAKIA

PALAIS MICHEL, LENINGRAD

Country Life

CALEDON, NORTHERN IRELAND

Country Life

PENRHYN CASTLE, WALES

THE DUOMO AND THE DUCAL PALACE, NEIGHBOURS ON AN ACROPOLIS

Ducal Palace, Urbino

The Renaissance ideal of a princely residence

FROM AFAR, across the plains of Tuscany and Umbria and up the Foglia valley, the ancient city of Urbino soars on its two hills above 'the Umbrian lakes smiling in summer heat, rich in crops, a land of generous fields'. To quote Propertius may not be absolutely in context, since Perugia, some miles from Urbino, was the poet's city. Still, from any approach, north, south, east or west, Urbino rises from the valley much as the golden pillars of Persepolis are sighted in the distant haze soon after leaving Shiraz. The impact of surprise in any approach to the city is as exciting as following the sound of music and finally arriving at its source.

It is a superb, mediaeval town dominated by towers and turrets, flying like pennants into the blue and white skies of its Umbrian painters. For 1,480 feet you climb up to the city, and through the narrow and crooked streets you follow always the road to the Duomo and the Palazzo Ducale, nextdoor neighbours to the huge central square. Wherever you are in the city these buildings stand supreme and dominate the whole.

The history of the Palazzo is, inevitably, bound by the history of the city and, as in most of the Italian city states of the Renaissance, by its rulers. Urbino, originally created capital of the Sabine Marches in the year 1000 (the Romans endearingly called it Urbinum Hortense – 'the little garden town') was ruled by the Montefeltro family

opposite: THE ENTRANCE COURTYARD, BY LUCIANO LAURAN

DUCAL PALACE, URBINO

who, in the fifteenth century, were Dukes of Urbino, and the Palazzo Ducale or Ducal Palace rivalled any of the courts of its greater neighbours of Milan, Florence, Venice or Perugia.

Federigo da Montefeltro, a benevolent ruler and patron of arts, had the whole palace, or fortress as it then was, redesigned and extended in 1465 by the Dalmatian architect, Luciano Laurana. The plans which they envisaged were to embody a 'city within a city', an ideal of many of the Renaissance humanist princes. In the patent which the Duke Federigo took out, he laid down that Laurana, 'a man more skilled in architecture founded upon arithmetic and geometry than any in Tuscany, that fountain of architects, must build in our city of Urbino a fair residence in all respects befitting the rank and reputation of our predecessors and ourselves'. In a setting of austere grandeur, 'proud, golden Urbino' as Dante called it, Federigo and Laurana built a superb palace of creamy Dalmatian limestone.

The front is built in a three-sided square. On each side of it rise tall, flanking towers which melt into turrets and spires. From the courtyard ascends a staircase of monumental proportions leading to the living-rooms – rooms vast and beautiful, small and magnificent, in which are housed the art treasures of The Marches, for the Palazzo is today the National Gallery of that district of Umbria. It was in

below: A CHURCH IS INCORPORATED IN THE FAÇADE

these rooms that the Duke Federigo founded his schools of art and poetry, mathematics and humanism. Right and left of the carriage entrance to the court are two rooms which were devoted to a library, more complete, according to Vespasiano, the Duke's librarian, than even those of Florence or of Oxford University. Every book had to be readily accessible, bound in silver-decked crimson and 'kept from the hands of dirty and tasteless persons'.

Among his distinguished citizens Federigo numbered Raphael and Bramante, and it is believed that here Piero della Francesca wrote his famous work, *The Science of the Perspective*. Alas, Urbino possesses only one painting by Raphael, her greatest son, and that, *Portrait of a Lady*, is in the large audience chamber. The collection of paintings which line the superb rooms of the palace is very fine, but the palace itself is the work of art which impresses most of all.

Federigo's household numbered 355 persons and there was stabling for 300 horses. This vast and beautifully preserved palace gives, even today, an impression of the bustle and activity of its long centuries of splendour. Perhaps not as great an architect as Bramante, Laurana was a master of the use of space and light. There is no gloom, no shadowy dark corners, no tortuous staircases throughout the whole palace. Here was light and enlightenment and a vigorous intellectual life as fine as that of the d'Estes at Ferrara or the Medicis in Florence. While Federigo might not have been a *pater patriae* as was Cosimo de Medici, he left behind him a legacy of learning and the encouragement of art of which the Palazzo Ducale is his greatest testament.

Laurana followed the Romans in his architectural style. From the classics he drew his love of light and his break-away from Gothic twilights and mediaeval gloom. He built the palace so that it appeared from the valley a forest of turrets and spires, and from the square a horizontal building, a domestic palace to be lived in. His courtyards are never square, the corners being rounded off by double pillars giving the impression of a curve.

All the rooms retain much of the florid magnificence, alternating with light delicacy, which distinguished Laurana's work. His choice of decorators to carry out his general conception of light allied to grandeur was a careful one, so that even unfurnished, as the rooms are today, they still retain their style. Each room is called by its ancient name and the use for which it was originally planned. The Hall of the Angels, designed by the Florentine, Domenico Rosselli, is a harmony of blue and gold against the plain Urbino stonework. The huge fireplace, decorated with angels designed by Botticelli, dominates the room. To give an impression of life and fluidity Laurana has here placed the tops of the windows, doors and fireplaces at irregular levels. This room was an ante-room to the throne room, and the door connecting the two rooms is the most important and beautiful in the whole palace. Based on designs by Botticelli, the carvings delicately reproduce the grace of the original drawings.

In the throne room, the largest in the palace, Laurana used a clever trick of lighting. All the windows face north, so that the light

TERRACOTTA PORTRAITS OF DUKE FEDERIGO DA MONTEFELTRO AND HIS SECOND WIFE, BATTISTA SFORZA

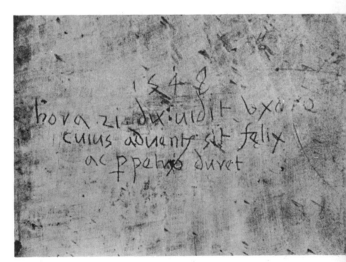

AN INSCRIPTION SCRATCHED ON A BALCONY IN 1548; THE DUKE REJOICES IN THE ARRIVAL OF HIS BRIDE

VIEW OF URBINO ON A COIN OF 1705

A MARQUETRY PANEL IN THE DUKE'S STUDY

adds a subdued elegance to the huge room. On the vaulted ceilings are the initials of F. C. (Federigo Comes) and on the walls the Lion of St Mark (for Guidobaldo was a Captain of the Serenissima) and the arms of Guidobaldo II.

The most beautiful room in the whole great palace is the *Studiolo* or study of the Duke Federigo. It is also the smallest. This was the Duke's own private room to which he retired for contemplation and studious pursuits. This very small chamber is sumptuously decorated with marquetry by Pontelli from drawings by Botticelli. The discreet and quiet lighting of this room is made more radiant by a finely carved ceiling embellished in vivid colours by Florentine artists. Here is a room which gives the immediate impression of being lived in. About the chamber are displayed numerous musical instruments, arms and books. Through a hidden door in the marquetry you reach the loggia which runs between the twin towers on the west side. From here a splendid panoramic view of the country-side stretches away to the distant mountains of the Abruzzi.

In one of the superbly vaulted rooms is a painting of the Duke Federigo and his young son, Guidobaldo. It was Guidobaldo who bequeathed the coronet of the Montefeltro family to that of the della Rovere, in 1508, and through them Urbino finally became a Papal State. So, the hill-fortress in which the Duke Federigo had gathered together in his own lifetime his great classical library, and from where he conducted internecine wars in a small way as a *condottiere* and patronised the arts and sciences in a most practical and encouraging fashion, found itself, two hundred years later, a fief of the Pope after the death of the last of the Urbino della Roveres.

Joyce Jeffreys

below: FEDERIGO'S STUDY, WITH TROMPE-L'ŒIL MARQUETRY BASED ON DESIGNS BY BOTTICELLI

DUCAL PALACE, URBINO

Laurana's work was prince

scale, but light and delicate

THE 'KING OF ENGLAND'S ROOM', NAMED AFTER JAMES STUART

THE THRONE-ROOM DISPLAYS
THE PURITY OF LAURANA'S ARCHITECTURAL LINES

left: THE SALA DEI ANGELI

25

DUCAL PALACE, URBINO

A PANEL OF THE DOOR TO THE THRONE-ROOM

right: A PANEL IN THE SALA DEI ANGELI

far right: DETAIL OF THE FIREPLACE IN THE DUKE'S
BEDROOM, BY DOMENICO ROSSELLI

The decorative
detail reveals
the Renaissance

CHÂTEAUDUN IN THE EIGHTEENTH CENTURY, BY J.-B. NESLE

Châteaudun

A fortress transformed into a palace

THE UNPRETENTIOUS TOWN of Châteaudun, twenty-seven miles
south of Chartres, spreads over rising ground on the south bank of
Le Loir, a little river not to be confused with its famous namesake,
La Loire, which flows through the heart of Touraine. At the east
end of the town the high ground ends in a rocky promontory, and
on this commanding site stands the castle of Châteaudun.

Nature here provided a strong-point on the northern boundary
of Touraine, and from far back into the Middle Ages it was occupied
by a fortress of great strength. The impregnability of the position
is not apparent on entering the courtyard from the town: fully to
appreciate the power and drama of the site, the building must be
seen from the old stone bridge crossing the river below the escarp-
ment. From this level the bastions and buttresses, with their foundations set on the living rock, soar upwards to the turrets and machi-
colations which crown the massive walls far above the roofs of the
town.

In the twelfth century, the famous family of Thibaut, counts of
Dunois, erected the robust circular keep, which stands at the south
end of the existing buildings. The structure was so massively built
that by almost no means, until the invention of high explosive, could
it have been demolished. The walls are more than twelve feet thick,
and are constructed in the fine, hard stone of the locality – as is the
whole of the château – which has now weathered to a mellow pearl-
grey. The dynasty of the Thibauts ended in 1218, and after passing

posite: THE TWELFTH-CENTURY KEEP AND GOTHIC CHAPEL

CHATEAUDUN

THE DUNOIS CHAPEL FROM THE STAIRCASE

A GOTHIC MULLIONED WINDOW

JEAN DUNOIS,
BASTARD OF ORLEANS

through female inheritance, the domain was bought by Louis of Or-léans, son of Charles V of France, in 1391. To the Orléans family is due the building of the château as it now exists.

Louis' illegitimate son, Jean Dunois, Bastard of Orléans, is one of the most romantic and revered figures in French history. In co-operation with Joan of Arc, he was eventually successful in expelling the English from all but a small area of France, and thus brought peace to his country after a century of turmoil. He was born in 1402, his mother being Henriette d'Enghien, so that in spite of illegitimacy he came from noble blood on both sides. From early years he was supporting his unworthy cousin, Charles VII, against the English, and for his inestimable services he was rewarded with a grant of the domain of Dunois, of which Châteaudun was the centre, and was also legitimised as of the blood royal.

The first work he undertook was the building of the chapel which, with the aid of his wife, Marie d'Harcourt, was begun in 1451. The exterior, with its simple Gothic lines, resembles many small chur-ches of the period, but the interior is given interest and distinction by the fifteen stone statues which ornament the walls. The name of the author of these sensitive sculptures is unknown, but they must date from the second half of the fifteenth century, and represent some of the finest work of the school of the Loire valley, of which Michel Colombe was the outstanding figure. The chapels on either side of the central apse have an unusual feature in the stone canopied fireplace which each contains, showing that Marie d'Harcourt realised that comfort was not incompatible with piety.

In 1453, the Hundred Years War at last reached its close, and the country was able to turn to the arts of peace. For the rich this normally meant rebuilding their fortress homes on more comfortable and domestic lines, an aspect which it had been impossible to deve-lop during the strife of the preceding decades. Dunois followed the prevailing example, and in 1460 began the long wing adjoining the chapel and the keep. It was still far from complete at his death eight years later. The design is plain, but the tall mullioned windows, provid-ing ample light and air to the spacious rooms within, were an innova-tion which came with an increasing sense of security. Nevertheless, above these purely domestic façades runs the mediaeval defence of the *chemine-de-ronde*, a covered passage corbelled out beyond the walls from which boiling liquids could be discharged onto attackers beneath. It is a feature to be found in châteaux built well into the following century, when its purpose had long since disappeared.

Although Dunois' building is plain within and without, it includes one magnificent piece of architecture – the splendid stone stair at the north-west angle. With its bold but delicate detail and graceful lines, it is as outstanding an example of the flamboyant Gothic style as was Dunois of the age of Chivalry. Both represent the final flower of their period. Usually the elaborate staircases, which were such a strik-ing feature of fifteenth and sixteenth-century châteaux, were contained in a tower, but at Châteaudun the circular stair is recessed into the building and gives onto galleries on each floor lighted by the open

opposite: THE GOTHIC STAIR FROM THE DOOR OF THE CHAPEL

CHATEAUDUN

tracery of the frontispiece.

After Dunois' death, his work was completed by his son François, Duc de Longueville. And thus the château remained until the latter's son, also François, began in 1511 an ambitious scheme for constructing two further wings, on the north and the west, which would have more than trebled the size of Dunois' building. In the event, only the north wing was erected, and this remains unfinished at its west end.

Important developments had taken place in the arts during the half-century since Dunois had begun his Gothic wing. The Renaissance style began slowly to penetrate into the indigenous Gothic style until eventually it entirely submerged it. The Longueville wing is an admirable example of this process in action. In its essential lines the new building showed little change from Dunois' wing, although it is conceived on a more grandiose scale, but into its decoration all manner of Renaissance detail is introduced. The openings on the splendid staircase have flattened arches, while classical motifs ornament the central pillar round which climb the broad stone steps.

The rooms within the Longueville wing are of greater size than those in the earlier building; indeed the Salle des Gardes and the Salle des Fêtes, one above the other, are more than one hundred feet in length. But in decoration they are austerely simple. There is a little stone carving on chimney-pieces and doorways, plain mouldings relieve the great wooden beams of the ceilings, some of the shutters are carved with a linen-fold design; but the walls are bare stone, and the tiled floors have a prophylactic aspect, which was no doubt

THE WALLS RISE LIKE CLIFFS FROM THE RIVER

below: THE SALLE DES GARDES OF THE LONGUEVILLE WING

highly desiderable in view of the insanitary manners of the times.

The unadorned walls now form an admirable background for a fine series of tapestries of the sixteenth and seventeenth centuries, while beneath them stand massive carved chests of much the same date as the building. Through the long windows of these great chambers there is a wide view northwards across the silver willows to the agricultural plain of La Beauce, which stretches away for more than twenty-five miles to Chartres.

To see the château in its serenity and excellent repair, it might be supposed that it had never suffered adversity. The reverse, however, is the truth, and it is miraculous that it has survived as anything but a ruin. From the Longueville family, which died out in the male line in 1694, the property passed by marriage to the Ducs de Luynes, with whom it remained until 1930. The first reverse to the château came in 1723, through the kindness of the owner in providing asylum for many families of the town rendered homeless by a fire. When the last of these guests eventually departed, the house was no longer habitable. Further damage was done during the Revolution, while in 1815, and again in 1870, it served the Prussians as a barracks. The building was thus brought to a condition which no private owner could remedy, and after sixty years of further decay the château was acquired by the State from the Duc de Luynes. Between 1948 and 1951 a faultless restoration was carried out by M. Trouvelot, architect of the Monuments Historiques.

Ralph Dutton

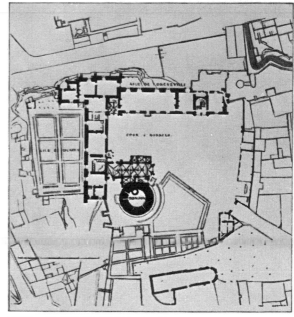

THE GROUND-PLAN SHOWS THE RELATION BETWEEN KEEP, CHAPEL AND THE TWO WINGS

FIFTEENTH-CENTURY STATUES IN THE CHAPEL

CHATEAUDUN

A GOTHIC MULLIONED WINDOW

The chief glory of Châteaudun is the Longueville staircase

THE STAIRCASE FROM THE COURTYARD

THE RIBBED VAULT COVERING THE STAIRCASE

ONE OF THE ARCHED GALLERIES

left: THE CENTRAL PILLAR OF THE SPIRAL STAIRCASE   35

THE UPPER TERRACE OF THE COURTYARD

Casa de Pilatos

Cool courtyards in the heart of Seville

THE CASA DE PILATOS (Pilate's House) is the Duke of Medinaceli's palace in Seville. It is so named because it is supposed to be a replica of the Praetorium of Pontius Pilate in Jerusalem. Begun at the end of the fifteenth century, it was not completed till 1570. It stands today as a perfect example of the house of a Renaissance nobleman.

The way to the house from the centre of Seville is an enchanting walk through a maze of winding and narrow streets. At every step one observes large houses, unpretentious from the front, but all graced by archways which give glimpses of cool courtyards heavy with palms and orange trees. Like most of these Sevillian houses, the Casa de Pilatos is unremarkable and even ordinary from outside. It is reached through an ill-kept courtyard preceding the main entrance, which is itself invisible from the street. In such a way have the discreet Dukes of Medinaceli kept themselves apart from the people of Seville.

This family, which has owned the house since it was built, is perhaps the most distinguished in all Spain – or even in Europe. They descend in the male line directly from an elder son a a thirteenth-century king of Castille, the weak but intelligent Alfonso the Wise, who died before his time, and whose sons were dispossessed by his brother, their wicked uncle. For several generations, the Dukes of Medinaceli (as they soon became – their title being taken from a small town north-east of Madrid) protested at every coronation in

opposite: A REPLICA OF PILATE'S PRÆTORIU

THE CARVED CEILING OF THE STAIRCASE

THE STAIRCASE, WITH ITS MUDÉJAR TILES

Spain that they were the rightful heirs to the throne. They were accordingly, and regularly, fined. But apart from these proud but ineffective protests, the Dukes of Medinaceli have not made a great impact upon the history of Spain. They have gathered to themselves many titles, among them those of Duke of Alcalá de Henares and of Luna and Marquis of Tarifa and of Camarasa. The Dukes of Medinaceli have always been among the foremost of those noblemen listed as grandees of Spain.

Besides the Casa de Pilatos the Duke of Medinaceli possesses five other great palaces in other parts of the peninsula. They have gathered enormous estates, especially in the classical provinces of *latifundia*, Andalusia and Estremadura. They are customarily in Seville for only twenty days a year, during the celebrated *Semane Santa* and its attendant *feria* and processions.

Walk through the outer archway of the Casa de Pilatos, cross an open space which hardly merits the name of courtyard, and stand briefly before the real main entrance to the house. This is a superb arch, rounded as if Romanesque but profusely decorated by delicate Moorish designs in stone. For the whole building, though begun over two centuries after the Christians captured Seville, was the work of mudéjar craftsmen-Moors, that is, Moors who worked under Christian masters. Through this archway, one can see the main courtyard of the Casa de Pilatos, with its marble floor, surrounded by smaller mudéjar arches. All of these are decorated with delicate patterns similar to those on the main arch. All the way round the courtyard runs an arched cloister, a marvellous gathering of glazed tiles, many of whose panels have the same concentrated beauty as the most dazzling of stained glass windows. In each corner of the court there are large statues of Latin writers, including an impressive figure of Seneca, who was born nearby in Cordoba. In the cloisters, a long series of busts of Roman emperors look outwards from niches near the roof. In the late sixteenth and early seventeenth centuries, when the Duke of Alcalá of that time made the Casa de Pilatos into an artistic salon, these busts were frequently copied by the young painters of Seville in search of a classical model. It is, indeed, not at all fanciful to suppose that those brilliant natives of Seville, Velázquez, Murillo and Zurbaran, may have studied beneath these glittering niches. Finally, in the middle of the courtyard, there stands an enigmatic head of the two-faced god, Janus, who, along with his Carthaginian colleague, Salammbo, was worshipped in Seville before the Romans came. (Both these gods were worshipped in Seville until well into the Christian era;

the two patron saints of the city, Saints Rufina and Justa, were two Christian women who refused to do reverence to Salammbo as her image was borne through the streets at the time of her festival, in July, commemorating the death of Adonis. They were therefore executed by order of the Roman governor, Diogenianus.

The rooms leading from the cloisters on the ground floor of the Casa de Pilatos are notable for their superb gilt and carved ceilings, all mudéjar. They are all also tiled in the same dazzling style as the cloisters. None of these rooms are now lived in. In the room on the right of the main entrance, two ancient but long unused coaches are preserved, in which the Dukes of Medinaceli would go to the Seville *feria* in the eighteenth century. From the windows of this room one can catch a glimpse of a rambling forest of orange and palm trees, accompanied by a maze of clematis and bougainvillea. Immediately opposite the main entrance of the Casa de Pilatos is the *sala de capilla*, the antechamber to the chapel. Here the Medinaceli family still waits before going into the chapel, and also passes the time of day afterwards. This room is furnished in the severe style of the Spanish seventeenth century.

Apart from the courtyard, the most striking feature of the Casa de Pilatos is the great staircase, four flights in length, very broad, and crowned by a gilt and carved cupola. The staircase itself is a masterpiece of brilliant tiling and immediately summons back the recollection of Seville during the golden sixteenth century. At the top of the stairs, a cloistered stone pathway runs all round the top of the courtyard, as a kind of gallery. From here, one can see, over the roofs of Seville, the top of the Giralda, the graceful Moorish campanile next to the cathedral, from which the muezzin, seven hundred years ago, would turn to the east and summon the faithful to prayer. Opening off this gallery, there are the bedrooms – and also a door leading to the present Duke of Medinaceli's private apartments. In addition, there is one long gallery, in the English sense of the word, filled with seals, charters and other documents belonging to the family. At the end of this room stands a superb painting of Mary Magdalene by Alvaro de Mena, a greatly underestimated Spanish fifteenth-century painter from Avila. An adjacent room is dominated by a vast genealogical tree of the Medinaceli family.

This house is a Renaissance jewel. It is sad that the Dukes of Medinaceli should choose to keep most of the treasures which were once housed in it in their architecturally much less interesting mansion in Madrid. *Hugh Thomas*

DON JUAN DE RIBERA

THE PRINCIPAL ROOM ON THE FIRST FLOOR

THE MARBLED FLOOR AND GLAZED TILES
OF THE INNER COURTYARD

39

A CEILING

A BACKGROUND OF BRILLIANT GREEN

MUDÉJAR TILES

Moorish in inspiration,
yet unmistakably
European

opposite: UNCHANGED, AND LITTLE DAMAGED, SINCE 15

THE QUADRATO IN THE EIGHTEENTH CENTURY

Villa Lante

Twin pavilions in a water-garden

THE SMALL VILLAGE of Bagnaia lies a mile or two from Viterbo, on the slopes of the Monti Cimini. At the upper end of the village is a small piazza with unpretentious buildings hung with the stone achievements of Popes' and Cardinals' arms. A heavily rusticated arch at the top of a short flight of curved steps, with a pediment surmounted by the Lante eagle, leads into the garden. We find ourselves on a terrace, a perfect square known as *Il Quadrato*. On three sides the garden is enclosed by box-hedges; at the corners of the fourth stand two matching pavilions of severely classical appearance. Carried on rusticated arcades, the *Piano Nobile* has three windows on each side, with pediments alternately pointed and round, set between pairs of pilasters. The presence of an upper floor is betrayed by a line of small windows below the tiled roof, from which rises an elaborate lantern, with pilasters, windows and blind arcades.

The Quadrato has two beds on each side planted with box-hedges in decorative patterns. In the centre is an elaborate water composition. Four basins, bordered by low parapets with vases, are arranged round a circle, reached by balustraded walks between the basins; the surface of the latter is broken by marine genii crouched in stone shells. Within the round centre, a raised circular basin contains the magnificent *Fontana dei Mori*, probably by Giovanni da Bologna: four life-sized figures of Moors, standing back-to-back in pairs with a lion between them, facing inwards towards the mounds and star of the Montalto arms which they hold aloft.

opposite: THE FOUNTAIN OF THE LAM

VILLA LANTE

CARDINAL GIANFRANCESCO GAMBARA,
WHO CREATED THE LARGER PART OF
THE GARDEN AND ONE OF THE PAVILIONS

The garden climbs a hill thickly wooded with oaks and ilexes, forming a movingly harmonious background to the Quadrato. But a moment passes before one realises that the parterre with its two pavilions is itself the Villa Lante, so far is it from accepted ideas of Renaissance palace. There is no attempt to startle or impress; even the central position has been abdicated in favour of the four Moors. The compelling quality of the Villa's beauty arises from its reticence and the simplicity of its basic design. The garden was normally a decorative adjunct to the palace, but here both garden and pavilions are planned, with complete success, as a single composition.

Both the unity of the design, and its masterly inspiration, make so strong an impression that it is paradoxical to learn that the architect is unknown, and that the Villa's construction was divided between two unrelated owners and spread over a period of about thirty years. Giovan Francesco Gambara, to whom the Villa is really due, came from an intellectual North Italian family. He was created Cardinal in 1561 and Apostolic Administrator of Viterbo in 1566, and seems to have started work at once on the Villa. Vignola must certainly have been known to Cardinal Gambara; and it seems to be generally agreed that the designs for the Villa and gardens were by him.

The Quadrato, the right-hand pavilion with Cardinal Gambara's name and his punning arms of a crayfish, and the upper garden, were all completed in a few years. The work however was then suspended and not resumed during Gambara's lifetime. He died in 1587 and was succeeded in the see of Viterbo by a nephew of the reigning Pope Sixtus V, Alessandro Peretti di Montalto, who had been created Cardinal two years earlier at the tender age of fifteen. The youthful Cardinal Montalto at once put in hand the Villa's completion. A second pavilion was added, in accordance with the original design. The loggia of the original, Gambara, pavilion has the walls frescoed with landscapes flanked by painted caryatids; the frescoes in the Montalto pavilion are by a later generation of artists. The young Claude Lorraine is said to have collaborated, as a student, in the latter's decoration.

below: THE MAIN ROOM OF THE MONTALTO
PAVILION

DETAIL OF THE CEILING OF THE MONTALTO PAVILION

The upper garden is planted with oaks, ilexes and plane trees in contrast to the open expanse of the Quadrato, but the two are ingeniously linked and the half-seen vistas of sculpture and fountains are most effective from below. In the centre of the first terrace, in a recess between two staircases, stands the *Fontana dei Lumini*. Replicas of Roman lamps set on the numerous ledges play small jets of water. Camellias, rhododendron and azaleas enliven the shade of the terrace. The chief feature of the third terrace is a long stone table with an open centre containing water which flows out through a grotesque mask at the lower end. Here Cardinal Gambara entertained his guests to *al fresco* meals. Against the middle of the far wall is a magnificent semi-circular fountain on three levels, flanked by huge bearded river-gods, Tiber and Arno, holding cornucopias and reclining against a mossy basin. Above this a crayfish (the Gambara arms), framed between two obelisks, projects a stream of water into a shell supported by a crouching slave. A double staircase ascends to the next terrace and the line of the stairs is continued to right and left by a row of columns. The fourth level of the garden is set on a gentle slope, crossed by a flight of shallow steps between box-hedges. Down the middle of the steps runs a *catena d'acqua*, a characteristic ornament of Renaissance gardens in Italy, found also at Villa d'Este and Caprarola.

In the centre of the terrace at the highest point of the garden, there is an elaborate octagonal fountain on five levels, crowned by a stemmed vase, ornamented with large dolphins, swags and grotesque masks and provided with a complicated system of jets. Other, hidden, jets were intended to play, unexpectedly (as at Villa d'Este) on the Cardinal's unwary guests. At the far end of the terrace a rocky grotto, half concealed by ferns and overhanging trees and flanked by two Atlas terms of primitive appearance and with the usual agonized expressions of their kind, is named the Fountain of Rain, or of the Flood. A small pavilion on either side completes a composition known as the Theatre of the Waters. These pavilions are simple but most distinguished; each has a tiled roof and an open loggia with a central arch carried on Ionic columns. Cardinal Gambara's name is engraved on the architrave and his arms are carved on both sides of the arch, the keystone being carved with a portcullis. Through the left-hand loggia one enters the 'Secret Garden', surrounded by hedges, low walls and lines of columns, which give it something of the atmosphere of a monastic cloister.

To the west of the garden, part of the original hunting reserve (still containing Cardinal Riario's modest hunting-lodge) seems to have been converted into a park in the sixteenth century. Its present form, however, evidently dates from a further transformation, no doubt in the late eighteenth century, into a *parco all'inglese*, but a number of fountains survive from the earlier period. Among these is the *Conservone* or reservoir, with a ledge decorated with a bust between two volutes and an extraordinary fountain composed of four contorted bearded masks.

The largest and most remarkable fountain at Bagnaia lies close below the Quadrato. This is the Fountain of Pegasus, an oval basin

THE LOGGIA OF THE GAMBARA PAVILION

KITCHEN IN THE GAMBARA PAVILION

THE QUADRATO, LOOKING TOWARDS BAGNAIA

THE CRAYFISH WAS THE GAMBARA CREST

surrounded on one side by a balustrade and on the other by a high balustraded wall against which are set busts of girls on top of huge consoles. In the middle is a superb figure of the winged horse.

After Cardinal Peretti's death Lante passed to Cardinal Ludovico Ludovisi, nephew of Pope Gregory XV, and then to Cardinal Antonio Barberini, nephew of Urban VIII. Innocent X bestowed it on Cardinal Federigo Sforza, and in 1656 Pope Alexander VII granted Lante to Duke Ippolito for himself and his descendants, a grant confirmed in the eighteenth century by Benedict XIV and in the nineteenth by Pius IX. We have a brief glimpse of the Villa in the latter part of the nineteenth century from Augustus Hare, who gives an inaccurate account of its history but pays tribute to the hospitality of the American Duchess, a daughter of Thomas Davis of New York. The Gambara pavilion, it seems, was occupied by the family, while the Montalto one was reserved for guests, and peacocks strutted up and down the avenues of the garden. Sir George Sitwell published a poetic description of the garden in 1909, but this was succeeded by a period of neglect and by more serious damage from Allied bombing in 1944 after the fall of Rome. Most fortunately, the Villa now belongs to Dr Angelo Cantoni, who has restored it, by a long process of admirably tactful repair, to its full beauty.

Anthony Hobson

opposite: THE ORIGINAL, GAMBARA, PAVILION, AND THE FOUNTAIN OF THE MOO

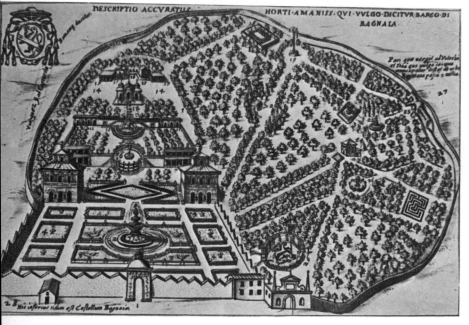

THE VILLA IN 1609, BEFORE THE FOUNTAIN OF THE MOORS WAS MADE

FOUNTAIN OF THE GIANTS

A BALUSTRADE OF STONE URNS

The three elements of Lante are stone, water and sculpture

opposite: THE FOUNTAIN OF THE MOORS, ATTRIBUTED TO GIOVANNI DA BOLOGN

left: THE FOUNTAIN OF PEGASUS

THE COURTYARD, WITH THE TÄNZL TABLET

Schloss Tratzberg

A Tirolean castle unspoiled by time

AS IT STANDS TODAY, Schloss Tratzberg in the Tirol can be said to date mainly from the beginning of the sixteenth century. The inscription emblazoned on the tower-stairs proudly recalls the year: '1500. Veit Jacob and Simon Tänzl, brothers, built the castle'. The year and the men mark the beginning of a new and artistically important chapter in the history of the castle. Whatever had gone before, it fell into oblivion. It had been a small boundary fortress where guards, bailiffs and tenants performed their general duties on the active north-south trade route that led across the valley of the Inn to the Brenner Pass and Italy. The site coud not have been better chosen for defence. The Inn did not flow steadily through the middle of the valley as it does today, but had to find a passage through boggy fields or between the rocks at the base of the fortress.

Tratzberg fell a victim to a fire in 1490 or 1491, and Maximilian, the future Emperor, who was sovereign of the province of Tirol, decided to leave the devastated castle to the two brothers Veit Jacob and Simon Tänzl, who belonged to one of the most esteemed and wealthy burgher families in Innsbruck. In rebuilding Tratzberg, they abandoned all unnecessary fortifications, and turned it into a palace in keeping with the new trends of their day. There is no doubt that the Tänzls were keenly aware of the flowering of the Renaissance in Italy, with which they had many trade relations. It

A COVERED STAIRWAY

VEIT JACOB TÄNZL AND HIS WIFE
ANNA: WOODEN STATUETTES IN THE
CHAPEL DATING FROM 1508

can be seen in the vast but harmonious composition of an unusual number of spacious rooms, and particularly in the magnificent furnishing and the use of rare materials. The beautifully chiselled marble doorways and columns, the skilfully ornamented locks and the metalwork on the doors and the carvings on the furniture and wainscottings still, however, retain some of the forms of the late Gothic. In two of the rooms, the so-called Maximilian rooms, the walls bear dates of the sixteenth and seventeenth centuries, partly recorded by the owners of the castle and partly by their guests, as if the walls were pages of a great family album. Crude frolics and wanton rhymes as well as serious reflections, speak for the hospitable character of the house. Even the noblest of their guests and their great patron, the Emperor Maximilian, here inscribed his own, melancholy musing:

> *Live, do not know how long.*
> *And die, do not know when.*
> *Must journey, do not know where.*
> *Wonder that I am so merry.*

The most famous work of art that Tratzberg retains from the time of the Tänzls is a family tree of the House of Hapsburg, a fresco that decorates the walls of the great hall. There are 148 portraits of half-length figures, and the work extends for 150 feet. It probably dates from about 1508. Below the fresco are seven powerful pairs of antlers, widely spaced from one another on the wall, and backed by large, painted stags. They were used as sconces for candles, and at night-time, the dark, powerful bodies of the stags and their softly illumined heads would emerge from the dimness of the wall between the princes and ladies of the Hapsburg genealogy.

Although they refused to employ the traditional fortifications in rebuilding their castle, the new owners did not leave themselves at the mercy of a surprise attack. Their castle gates were flanked with embrasures for cannon and the strong castle walls were easily convertible to defence. A number of secret exits were constructed for sudden escape in time of emergency. One of the beautiful living-rooms of the Tänzls has a secret winding staircase hidden in the thickness of the wall leading by an underground passage into the open.

The property passed to Simon Tänzl's son, Caspar Joachim, whose passage is recorded by an inlaid crest in the panelling of the Tänzl room. But, owing to business losses, he was obliged to sell the castle, and in 1554 it passed into the hands of a wealthy Augsburg patrician, George Ilsung, who was related to the lord of the Tirol, the Archduke Ferdinand. What the Tänzls had initiated half a century earlier was now to be completed. Tratzberg became a Renaissance palace. Ilsung built the north wing and a Renaissance façade to it extending along the hillside, and enclosing the courtyard. Inside, he redecorated the rooms, creating in the Queen's room, in the style of the Flemish late Renaissance, one of the most wonderful features of its kind in Austria. It is said that it took seven carpenters and seven apprentices seven years and seven months to construct the coffered ceiling with its carved beams and panels. The sense of comfort and splendour in this room is heightened by the beautifully woven material that hangs

THE ARMOURY   A BEDROOM OF THE ILSUNG PERIOD   NINETEENTH-CENTURY HUNTING GROUP

flat against the walls between elaborate framed doors and cupboards.

From 1589 to 1657 Tratzberg was owned by the celebrated Augsburg family of Fugger. But it had seen the best of its days with the passing of the Ilsungs. Though Jacob Fugger indeed made some additions to the castle, no fundamental changes were made by him or his descendants. The incomes of the new owners no longer sufficed for the upkeep of the castle on such an extensive scale as their predecessors. So they chose to live only at rare intervals in the big, old house. The priest's apartments continued to be occupied both privately and officially, when Tratzberg became a priory in 1700 for young men destined to the priesthood, but the modest requirements of successive priors and the restricted means of its owners saved the castle from the decorative tastes of the Baroque period. When the priory was abandoned in 1790, Tratzberg fell into a sleep from which it was only roused in 1809 and 1810 by young patriots from the neighbouring village who broke into the famous armoury to equip themselves for their fight against the French.

When Tratzberg was acquired in 1847 by the present owners, the Counts Enzenberg, the castle again received all the love and care it deserved. The first of them, Count Franz Enzenberg, refused to be influenced by the new zeal of the Romantic movement, which might have found in Tratzberg a perfect setting for neo-Gothic treatment, and thus preserved the character of the castle for his descendants. The large hunting groups, by the well-known carver Toni Steger, date from his time. Today, Tratzberg faces a landscape steeped in the traditions of the past, but in the peaceful atmosphere of the courtyard there is no sign or sound of hustle.

Franz Windisch-Graetz

MANUSCRIPT OF 1508
RECORDING THE CONSECRATION
OF THE CHAPEL

TRATZBERG

THE TÄNZL INSCRIPTION ON THE TOWER

INSCRIPTION BY THE EMPEROR MAXIMILIAN —
'AND DIE, DO NOT KNOW WHEN'

The history of the house is

DETAIL OF THE EARLY SIXTEENTH-CENTURY HAPSBURG FAMILY-TREE

56   *right:* THE HAPSBURG FAMILY-TREE IN THE GREAT HALL

corded on its walls

A DOOR FROM THE FUGGER PERIOD, 1589-1657

Each generation has left its legacy to the castle

opposite: THE QUEEN'S ROOM, LATE SIXTEENTH CENTURY

below: AN OCTAGONAL TURRET ROOM

Prospetto del Regio Ducal Palazzo del Te

Palazzo del Te

'Chambers of transgression, now forlorn!'

THE PALAZZO DEL TE is surely of all Renaissance buildings the easiest to understand and to enjoy. As you approach it through the untidy modern suburbs of Mantua, standing there by itself, four-square on the fringe of the marshes, like a flat box of brown-gold stone, you feel that you can take it in at a glance. And so, indeed, you can: its design is simple, its scale is small, it is all of a piece. Simple also was the way it came into being: it was built entirely for the purposes of pleasure and completed in little more than a decade under the direction of a single architect. Neither later generations not 'the unimaginable touch of time', though they have drained its fish-ponds and stripped it of its ornaments, have by addition or subtraction altered the lucid design or maimed the perfect structure.

It was in 1524 that Federigo, son of Isabella d'Este, the second ruling Gonzaga of his name, fifth Marchese and later first Duke of Mantua, decided to build himself a pleasure-dome outside the walls of the city. Its design and execution were entrusted to Raphael's pupil Giulio Romano, with a troop of painters, sculptors, plasterers and gilders working under him. The building itself was erected within eighteen months; then the decorators set to work, and for the next ten years a pattern of frescoes, carvings and plaster-work crept round the walls and ceilings of the four sides of the *cortile*.

The progress of the work can be traced in the Gonzaga archives, which preserve a series of letters addressed by Federigo to his architect, commending his performance or chiding his delay, and a mass of documents recording payments made for work done.

opposite: INSIDE THE LOGGI

PALAZZO DEL TE

No artist of the first rank worked under Giulio. Among his assistants were the architect Giambattista Covo; for sculpture and plaster work, Francesco Primaticcio; for fresco, Benedetto Pagni and Rinaldo Mantovano. A score of lesser-known names occur in the accounts, but Giulio was the principal contributor and what he did not himself execute he designed and controlled.

'Pleasure-dome' is perhaps too grand a name for Giulio's creation; it is too modest for that both in scale and in design. Rather, it is a summer-house; yet it has nothing of the lightness, the trivial elegance of the Trianons; it is solid and dignified; almost, in its outward aspects, severe. The lay-out consists of a quadrangle, its measurement some thirty yards each way, enclosed by a range of single-storey buildings made of golden stone. Round the inner façades of this *cortile*, just under the roof-line, runs a frieze, broken into a series of metopes and supported by pairs of engaged Doric columns. Few windows look into the courtyard: only four on the northern side and six on the southern, and the eastern and western sides are almost blind. The columns are separated by deep niches, and the intervening surfaces are fretted with *spezzato* treatment, giving depth and life to the solidity of the stone façades.

The entrance is through a simple gateway that pierces the middle of the western side; an answering archway on the east leads to a *loggia* from which you look out over a pair of deep rectangular fish-ponds which abut, like a moat, upon the outer side of the eastern façade. Before you lies a stretch of garden ground, enclosed by a plain wall on either side and terminated about a hundred and fifty yards away by a tall *esedra*, a semicircle of rounded arches, like a fragment of a Roman aqueduct, against which, falling across the level garden, strike the rays of the setting sun.

In the left-hand corner of the garden is the *Casino della Grotta*, a cluster of rooms enclosing a tiny 'secret garden', with a *logetta* and a grotto where courtiers and guests could bathe in a little cascade of water that made music as it fell over the shells and pebbles that encrust the walls.

The external aspect of the palace has altered little since it was built. The courtyard has lost its flag-stones; the formal garden, once, no doubt, a labyrinth of topiary patterns, is now a waste of grass; the plaster has peeled from the *esedra*; the frescoes have vanished from the walls, and the fountains play no longer in the empty fish-ponds; but the low *cortile*, its back to the setting sun, still stretches its long arms around the garden, to meet in a hand-clasp by the arched *esedra* at its eastern end.

In the interior, which depended for effect largely upon perishable ornament, the change has been greater. It has exposed the simplicity of the internal design — or, rather, the lack of any design at all. For the palace is no more than a single chain of rooms, half-a-dozen or so on each of the four sides, none of them much more than thirty feet across, leading one out of the other round the four sides of the *cortile*. All are on the ground floor; there is not a staircase or a passage-way to be seen. In all these rooms nothing remains of past

PART OF A LETTER FROM GIULIO ROMANO TO HIS PATRON, MARCHESE FEDERIGO, 31 AUGUST 1528, EXCUSING HIMSELF FOR THE DELAYS IN COMPLETING THE FRESCOES AT THE PALAZZO. THE LETTER READS: 'The greatest affliction I can receive is when Your Excellency is annoyed. The greatest glory I can know is when I can feel myself to be in your favour. And if it be Your Grace's pleasure, you may lock me up in that big room until it is finished'.

THE ESEDRA THROUGH THE ARCH
OF THE LOGGIA

splendour save the fine marble fire-places, the frescoes and moulded plasterwork that still cling to the upper walls and ceilings, and a few inscriptions along a frieze or over a doorway, doing honour to Federigo in grand Roman letter and strange Renaissance Latin. The doorways have lost their doors of bronze or carved wood, the walls have been stripped of their tapestries; the gilt has vanished from the mouldings, and all the furnishings that made it once a place of luxury and delight have disappeared: every room in the voluptuous palace is entirely bare.

In all this chain of rooms – the *Sala di Psiche*, the *Stanza del Sole*, the *Stanza delle Metamorfosi*, the *Sala delle Medaglie*, the *Sala di Cesare*, the *Sala di Fetonte* – there are only two that achieve more than a merely decorative effect; for the rest, the *Sala di Psiche* may stand as representative. That famous room shows Giulio at his most lavish: Ovid and Apuleius have come to life; gods and satyrs and nymphs and Bacchanals riot in an unbroken Olympian tapestry over the walls and vaulted ceiling. If it proves that Giulio was an inventive and accomplished decorator, it also suggests that he was nothing more. Not a scene, not a figure, has a life or dignity or beauty of its own; none dwells in the memory like those with which his master Raphael ennobled the *Stanze* in the Vatican or his rival Mantegna the walls of Federigo's ducal palace. Even as a decorator, Giulio cannot boast the splendour of Veronese or the swagger of Tiepolo.

The exceptions are the *Sala dei Giganti* and the *Sala dei Cavalli*. The *Sala dei Giganti* stays in the memory, but only for its grotesque effects: *non si pensi alcuni*, says Vasari, *di vedere opera di pennello piú orribile e spaventosa di questa*. Here Rinaldo Mantovano has portrayed the downfall of the giants who tried to scale Olympus (not without a side-glance, perhaps, at any who might have designs against the house of Gonzaga): the whole small room – it is only thirty-six feet square – is tumbling about one's ears: ceiling, windows, doors, by a series of *trompe-l'œil* devices, are involved in the ruin, and the grotesque giants, like swollen dwarfs, struggle in vain contortions.

The *Sala dei Cavalli*, on the other hand, though it too is unique, impresses not as a curiosity but as a work of art. The room is the largest in the palace; it has a fine marble fire-place and an elaborate coffered ceiling; the walls are painted in *grisaille* with *trompe-l'œil* statues in niches between Corinthian columns. But the thing that dominates the whole chamber is Rinaldo's series of life-size portraits (for that they are actual portraits one cannot doubt) of six splendid horses. They stand at window-height, breaking the painted architectural framework they are placed in; patient and powerful, the one piece of rounded breathing reality in the room – or, indeed, in the whole palace. They record the glories of the Gonzaga breed of horses: Federigo's stables adjoined the palace, and just beyond the *esedra* still stands a training-stable, where, peering through the arches, one can see the thoroughbreds at exercise; alive, but no more real than their painted ancestors within.

On a summer's day it is not hard to picture the Gonzaga Court

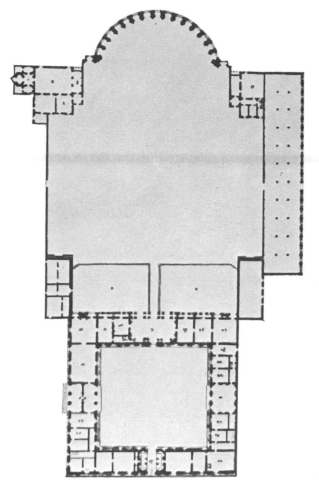

THE GROUND-PLAN SHOWS THE SQUARE COURTYARD ENCLOSED BY THE MAIN HOUSE, AND THE GARDEN TERMINATED BY THE SEMI-CIRCULAR ESEDRA

THE EASTERN FAÇADE OF THE LOGGIA (9 IN PLAN)

CEILING OF THE GROTTO IN THE CASINO DELLA GROTTA

assembled on the *loggia* to receive some Royal or Imperial visitor –
as the Emperor Charles V himself was there received in 1530, when
the Dukedom of Mantua was conferred upon his host – or taking
their ease in the garden, 'listening to music, to the reading of Ban-
dello's novels, to the sound of water, to time as it flies'.

Throughout the High Renaissance these delights continued, to
be brought to a frightful end after a century. It was in 1630 that
Mantua fell before the combined assault of the Imperial forces and
one of the most terrible plagues in history, and, with the rest of the
city, the Palazzo del Te was put to the sack.

After the Imperial troops had worked their will, nothing of all
its splendour remained but what we see today. And it is perhaps in
autumn, when the mists are rising from the marshes, that the desert-
ed palace inspires the most genuine emotion, bringing to mind a line
from Wordsworth that might almost have been written to describe
it: 'Chambers of transgression', one murmurs as one paces the desolate
apartments, 'Chambers of transgression, now forlorn!'.

John Sparrow

GIULIO ROMANO'S OLYMPIAN BANQUET IN THE SALA DI PSICHE

left: THE SALA DELLE MEDAGLIE

above: A DETAIL OF THE SAME ROOM

THE SALA DEI CAVALLI

Horses and giants in the Palazzo del Te

opposite: THE SALA DEI GIGANTI

Chambord

A French château of ingenious vastness

ENGLAND HAS BEEN unfortunate in losing the remarkable palace with which Henry VIII endeavoured to introduce the style of the Renaissance into his country. Nonsuch is now no more than a name. France, however, has been more lucky; and François I's Château de Chambord, which was begun sixteen years earlier than Nonsuch, still stands ten miles east of Blois with its structure intact. Lying within a great domain encircled by a ten-foot wall twenty miles in length, it still presents the appearance its founder envisaged.

François did not choose a virgin site; a fortified structure had stood here from which Joan of Arc set out for the siege of Orleans. The King, however, had no strategic consideration in mind; his building was to be purely a *Maison de plaisance* – a centre for hunting and for relaxation from the affairs of state. It was indeed to be a hunting box, the finest of its sort ever constructed. In the event, it remained for two centuries third in importance of the royal palaces, being exceeded only by Versailles and Fontainebleau, though after the extinction of the Valois line on the death of Henri III in 1589 it was used decreasingly as a residence.

The site is low-lying, but well adapted to François' purpose. The thickly wooded country provided the best hunting in Touraine, and the little river Cosson supplied water to fill the moat with which the château was to be surrounded. In 1519, four years after François had ascended the throne, the enterprise was begun.

opposite: THE WIDE TERRACE ON WHICH THE CHÂTEAU STAND: BOUNDED BY THE RIVER COSSON

CHAMBORD

A DRAWING OF FRANCIS
I BY HIS COURT PAINTER
CLOUET

The arts had not blossomed freely during the reign of the preceding King, Louis XII, but François was well aware that beyond the Alps movements were in progress by the standards of which the arts in France remained at a deplorably low level. From the first he was determined to make his court a centre of culture which could rival that of Italy; and to this end he induced many artists, sculptors and men of letters to leave Italy for France. Even the great Leonardo da Vinci was persuaded in 1516 to bring his illumination to the valley of the Loire at Amboise. It is generally supposed that one of these exponents of Italian culture, Domenico da Cortona, provided the original plans. If so, the design must have been radically altered as building proceeded, for the château emerged as an inherently French conception and is the most splendid example of French Renaissance architecture in the country.

The usual approach is from the north, along one of the wide rides through the farm lands and forests of the domain, and the first sight of the château at the end of an avenue is supremely dramatic. The massive structure with its elaborate crown of turrets and cupolas has an outline as delicate in its filigree detail as the leaves of the trees themselves; while the pale Bourré stone in which it is built – retaining an astonishing, even excessive, freshness of colour – adds to the sensational effect. From this north aspect, with the long façade punctuated by four robust circular towers, the true form of the building is not apparent, but this becomes clear on passing to the entrance on the south side, where a single-storeyed range encloses a rectangular courtyard. Here it can be seen that the central section of the château is in the form of that traditional feature of French mediaeval buildings, a keep – a keep of cyclopean proportions, with a huge round tower at each corner. The wings, which extend the north façade to

THE SOUTH FAÇADE

such immense length, are shallow three-storeyed galleries connecting the keep to the outlying towers at the east and west ends.

This plan hardly seems one to have come from an Italian architect, and yet the arrangement of the keep incorporates a typically Italian feature. Each of the three main floors is divided by galleries in the form of an equal-armed Greek cross into four corner divisions. Each division forms a complete apartment consisting of two spacious rooms, one in the main block, one in the corner tower, with a number of small rooms for servants reached by a spiral stair. This apartment plan which was early abandoned in Italy, continued in French châteaux for upwards of two centuries.

At the central point rises the staircase which, with the fantastic decorations of the roof, is the outstanding feature of Chambord. It is undoubtedly one of the triumphs of the Renaissance. Twin sets of wide stone steps, entwined but never meeting, lead upward by gentle gradations within an open cage of massive stone pilasters. Here there is none of the barbaric exuberance of design found on the roof, but instead there is an admirable purity and restraint in decoration. And yet it is so essentially a French production that its designer can hardly have been Italian. From this beautiful structure – now so useful for conducting hordes of visitors over the château – one emerges onto the roof into a riot of stone decoration and carved ornament. A riot, indeed, it at first appears, but in fact the main masses and the opulent detail is disposed and ordered on the strictest rules of symmetry. The corner apartments, as on the lower floors, rise here from the terrace, on to which their doors open, thus forming probably the earliest examples of pent-houses. Their roofs are covered with fine grey-blue slates, against which are outlined dormer windows with elaborate crestings, tall chimney stacks, and circular turrets containing spiral stairs. All are lavishly, in fact recklessly, decorated with classical ornaments borrowed from the buildings and textbooks of Italy. Above this tumult rises to a height of one hundred feet the lantern and cupola crowned with a fleur-de-lys.

It was improbable that so huge and elaborate a building could be completed within the reign of one monarch, particularly as in this case operations were discontinued between 1524 and 1526 when François was in captivity in Italy. However, on his return to France, work was begun again with renewed vigour. An army of eighteen hundred workmen was employed on construction and, in 1537, the keep was roofed, while two years later the east wing was covered. The west wing, however, was not completed till 1550, three years after François' death, and some works were still in progress in 1571. Since that time no material alterations have been made to the fabric, except for the addition by Louis XIV of an attic floor to the single-storeyed buildings surrounding the court; but this was removed a few years ago.

Louis XIV, in the earlier years of his reign, paid several visits to Chambord and for him the rooms on the first floor of the north front of the keep were rearranged. By closing the northern arm of the cross, two corner apartments were united so that a fine suite of rooms was provided for the royal use. Simple *boiseries*, with tapestries

RENAISSANCE DETAIL SEEN THROUGH AN ARCH

THE SOUTH-WEST TOWER OF THE KEEP

and pictures, now give these rooms an agreeable domestic quality which is far from prevalent in the cold stone halls of the remainder of the château. Louis XV was little attracted to the place, the robust architecture of which was sharply out of tune with the delicate taste of the period. He was doubtless happy to be able to offer it to his father-in-law, Stanislas Leckzinski, who had inconveniently come to France on being ousted from his kingdom of Poland. Here the ex-king, suffering severely from rheumatism, for which reason he suppressed the moat, spent a number of gloomy years until he was made governor of Lorraine. There, at Nancy, he was able happily to indulge his taste for pure eighteenth-century classicism in creating the exquisite square which bears his name.

Soon after Stanislas' departure from Chambord, another occupant surprisingly appeared in the person of the Maréchal de Saxe. This illustrious figure, an illegitimate son of the Elector of Saxony, and one of the most successful generals in the service of France, received a grant of the château in 1748. Here he carried on a train of life almost regal in style, but in 1750 he died suddenly – worn down, it was said, more by the ardours of love than of war. Chambord was never again fully occupied.

At the Revolution the château, which had returned to the Crown, suffered the usual damage; everything moveable – furniture, doors, panelling – was either sold or burnt, while the dismantled structure was used as a prison. It must have been with misgivings that Maréchal Berthier received the estate with the title of Prince de Wagram from Napoleon in 1809. Small in stature and unaccustomed to a life of grandeur, Berthier was singularly ill-suited to the vast rooms of Chambord, and he seldom attempted to live there. 'Quittez ce triste Chambord', he wrote in April 1814 to his wife, who had retired there with their children; and less than fourteen months later Berthier died, falling from a window in the palace at Bamberg – having been driven to suicide, it was supposed, by the agonies of divided loyalties during the Hundred Days.

The Princesse de Wagram had not the means nor the wish to restore and maintain the château, and in 1821 the estate was bought from her by public subscription, and given to the infant grandson and heir of Charles X, who was henceforth known as the Comte de Chambord. At the revolution of 1830, the young prince left France with the rest of the royal family, and did not re-enter the country till forty-one years later, when, after the repeal of the law of exile against the Orleans family, he came to Paris and on 2nd July, 1871 to Chambord – his only visit. His refusal to accept the Tricolor banished all hopes of restoration, and three days later he left France again for ever. At Chambord are preserved various pathetic objects prepared for his triumphal entry into Paris as Henri V; the satin-lined coach is in the hall, and in the little church on the adjacent slope are various panels of needlework finely stitched by the women of France with the arms of the Comte and his wife. The Prince died in 1883, and in 1930 the château and domain were acquired by the State from his heirs, the Princes of Bourbon-Parme.

Ralph Dutton

A DORMER-WINDOW IN THE EAST WING

THE RECONSTRUCTED BEDROOM OF LOUIS XIV

osite: THE BED-ALCOVE OF LOUIS XIV

THE VILLA STANDING ABOVE THE FOUNTAIN OF THE DRAGONS

Villa d'Este

A Cardinal's villa among the cypresses and cascades

THE PRESENT ENTRANCE to the Villa d'Este is a modest doorway off a piazza in the town of Tivoli, in an angle beside the Church of San Francesco. Through a passage one reaches a cobbled courtyard, with vaulted arcades of great beauty and simplicity round three sides, resembling a Florentine cloister of the Quattrocento. Only a grotto on the fourth side, with a figure of a sleeping Venus, recalls the High Renaissance when this former Benedictine Abbey was transformed into a Cardinal's palace.

On the garden side of the courtyard is a series of high rooms. One of these has its original coved ceiling, decorated with frescoes and stucco; another has a painted coffered ceiling with the arms and crest of Cardinal Ippolito d'Este, the builder of the Villa. On a lower floor, reached by an internal staircase and a passage with grottoes and fountains, is a further series of rooms. The central hall is particularly successful, frescoed with arabesques and classical figures.

The garden façade is plain to the point of monotony. Its sole architectural feature is an arched portico in the centre, in two storeys, with Doric columns below and Corinthian above. From the upper portico a double staircase leads down to a broad balustraded terrace, on which the lower portico stands, containing a grotto with a figure of Minerva. From the terrace one can for the first time appreciate the full beauty of the Villa's position. We are on a hillside,

opposite: A SUBTLE COMPLEX OF PATHS AND STAIRWAYS LEADS TO THE GARD

THE PORTICO ON THE UPPER TERRACE

THE FOUNTAIN OF THE ORGAN

the first height above the plain that stretches beyond Rome. To the right are the pink walls and red tiled roofs of Tivoli, and the mulberry campanile of its cathedral. Below us are the giant cypresses, the towering ilexes, the oleanders, lemon trees and agapanthus of the garden, an infinite variety of greenness and shade. And from every side comes the sound of running water.

The first set-piece, the 'Way of a Hundred Fountains', is a paved walk parallel with the Villa's façade and extending the full width of the garden. The upper side is lined with three long narrow basins. A row of stone fountains, in the form of the eagles and fleurs-de-lys of the d'Este arms, alternating with obelisks and urn-shaped boats, lines the lip of the topmost basin. The eagles spew water from their mouths with a contemptuous expression, the other emblems shoot it upwards and sideways, while other jets fall into the middle, creating patterns as delicate as the tracery of Gothic architecture, more magical in their change and movement. At one end of the *Viale delle Cento Fontane* is the *Rometta*, a model of ancient Rome. At the other end, is the majestic oval of the *Fontana dell'Ovato*. This is built against the hillside on two levels. Gigantic figures of two river-gods and of the Tiburtine Sybil loom mysteriously from shaded cavities in a vast grotto surmounted by Pegasus in the act of striking Parnassus with his hoof. From the grotto three cascades fall to pass below a curved terrace.

From the middle of the 'Hundred Fountains', runs the central axis of the garden. Two sphinxes are crouched at the top of a magnificent curved double stairway, water shoots from their breasts ('in limpid but impure jets', observes Dr De Vita in the admirable official guide to the Villa) and is carried in a *catena d'acqua* down the balustrade of the stairs. The arms of the staircase, meeting above at an arched grotto of golden stone with Ionic columns and joined at the foot by a low parapet, enclose the Fountain of the Dragons. Legend has it that this was inspired by the Buoncompagni arms and built in a single night in honour of a sudden visit by the Pope of that family, Gregory XIII. Around a great central vertical jet are grouped four dragons; real creatures of the Pleistocene, low-browed and ageless, strayed from some primaeval swamp to squat eternally, spewing water into the basin round them with the full concentration of their pea-sized minds.

The last set-piece comprises three rectangular basins, with vases on the parapets playing thin jets. At one end, against the cliff on which the town of Tivoli stands, the superposed fountains of Neptune and the Organ form a single grandiose composition of falling sheets of water and jets rising from different levels in heights increasing towards the centre. Inside an arch at the foot, a muscular Neptune is half seen through his native element. The upper fountain starts from a monumental arch standing on a terrace. It is in two storeys, surmounted by a broken pediment with the d'Este eagle in the centre. A circular clearing planted with cypresses beyond the three basins is a vantage-point to look backwards up the garden. The austerity of the Villa's façade, familiar from a famous series of drawings by

Fragonard, is hidden by trees; only the portico stands out, aligned above the Dragons at the top of a flight of steps.

Cardinal Ippolito d'Este was born in 1509, son of Alfonso I, Duke of Ferrara, and of Lucrezia Borgia. Archbishop of Milan at the age of ten, Cardinal at thirty, son of an Italian ruler, grandson of a Pope, he hoped in vain for the Papacy. Fobbed off with the empty distinction of Governor of Tivoli, he sought in building consolation for the ruin of his ambitions. Immediately after the Cardinal's state entry into Tivoli in 1550, the Neapolitan architect Pirro Ligorio was commissioned to convert a disused Benedictine monastery into a suitable residence.

The first years were fully occupied in clearing the site. Vineyards, olive groves and about forty houses were destroyed to make the garden, not without complaints from the Cardinal's new subjects. A tunnel was dug through the hill to harness the waters of the River Aniene to the fountains, and an aqueduct was built to carry the water from Monte Sant'Angelo below the courtyard, in order to operate the highest jets. During the Pontificate of Pope Paul IV, Cardinal d'Este was obliged to retire to Ferrara, and it was not till 1560 that a new period of intense activity opened. Inside the Villa, Federigo Zuccaro, Livio Agresti and Gerolamo Muziano, with their respective pupils, were at work on the frescoes, together with a team of *stuccatori*. Excavations were set on foot on Hadrian's Villa below the Tivoli hill to supply antique statues for the house and garden. In 1571 it was estimated that two years would be enough to finish the work, but the Cardinal died the next year and his grandiose scheme has never been completed.

Cardinal Ippolito left the Villa to the Cardinals of his family, or in default of any, to the Deacon of the College of Cardinals. Cardinals Luigi and Alessandro d'Este enjoyed it in turn; after the latter's death in 1624, the d'Estes, Dukes of Modena, secured from Pope Urban VIII a reversal of the will and the gift of the property to them. Under their remote supervision the Villa suffered from progressive neglect, accentuated when it passed, through Maria Beatrice d'Este, wife of the Archduke Ferdinand, to the Hapsburgs. The sculptures were filched or removed, the water-channels became choked, the stonework crumbled and fell. In the latter half of the last century it enjoyed an Indian summer under the care of Cardinal Hohenlohe, who was in charge au Austrian representative at the Vatican. Liszt was given a suite of rooms in the Villa in 1865 and spent part of each year there for the remaining twenty years of his life. There it was that he took refuge – for although by then sixty and in holy orders, he was still by no means unattractive to women – from the infatuation of Olga Janina, a passionate Cossack Countess of nineteen: in vain, however, as she gained admission disguised as a gardener's boy. As memories of Liszt's residence we have his two evocative compositions, *Cyprés de la Villa d'Este* and *Jeux d'eau de la Villa d'Este*. In 1917 the Villa was confiscated as enemy property by the Italian State.

Anthony Hobson

A FOUNTAIN INSIDE THE VILLA

SLEEPING VENUS IN THE ENTRANCE COURTYARD

COAT-OF-ARMS OF CARDINAL IPPOLITO D'ESTE

VILLA D'ESTE

THE 'HUNDRED FOUNTAINS'

THE FOUNTAIN OF THE DRAGONS IS SAID TO HAVE
BEEN CREATED IN A SINGLE NIGHT

right: THE SUPERIMPOSED FOUNTAINS
OF NEPTUNE AND THE ORGAN

The wate

MONTAIGNE COMPARED THE FOUNTAINS TO GIANT MECHANICAL TOYS

reates an architecture of its own

THE GARDEN WAS LAID OUT IN THE 1730'S

Egeskov

The proud memorial of a Danish nobleman

THE DANES BELIEVE THAT great houses are all the better for being lived in, if possible by the family which has owned them for generations past. So it is with many of the great manorhouses of Denmark, and so it is today with Egeskov. Since the first farmhouse was built on this site in 1405, Egeskov has had thirty-two masters. In 1533 the name Bille first appears as that of an owner of Egeskov. About 1616 Jakob and Frantz Ulfeldt owned the estate, and today it is the property of Count Gregers Ahlefeldt-Bille.

From the village of Kvaerndrup a noble avenue of limes leads the visitor to a causeway, which spans a short neck of water, and to the west door of the castle. On the eastern front the warm, ancient brick of two semi-circular towers is reflected from the little lake. This sheet of water, which today gives Egeskov much of its almost unique attraction, was, however, no whim of a rich patron or his landscape gardener. This site was chosen for defence, by Frands Brockenhuus, who acquired Egeskov by marriage in 1545. He appointed Martin Bussert as his architect for the castle which he at

THE MOST BEAUTIFUL MANOR-HOUSE IN DENMARK

left: TOMB OF THE BROCKENHUUS AT KVAERNDRUP
right: THE WOODEN MAN IN THE LOFT

once set himself to build. Bussert was the pioneer of Renaissance architecture in Denmark, but, like his employer, he was also a notable soldier, and had a keen eye for military needs in an unsettled time. The castle was built on oaken piles, driven into the bed of a small lake, and could be approached originally only by a complicated system of drawbridges. The main shell of the castle is composed of two buildings, separated by a wall seven feet thick, riddled with secret passages, staircases and what we should now perhaps call booby traps. A suspension bridge gives access to the east front of the castle, but the main entrance is, as it has always been, on the western side. An elaborate portico which was erected in front of this ancient doorway in 1880, was demolished thirty years ago, leaving the west front as it was designed, more than four hundred years before.

This great mansion is not an ancient monument, though officially classified as one by the Danish Government. It is not a sterile box, handsomely furnished and equipped in the manner of a past age but no longer a part of this one. It is a home. The portraits are there – Niels Krag, who laid out the garden, Admiral Steen Bille, who brought back from St Helena a willow which he had taken from Napoleon's grave, and which grew and flourished at Egeskov until twenty years ago, and those of a hundred others who had lived at Egeskov and loved it. But these hang with the trophies brought home by the present owner, who is one of the world's most celebrated big-

THE EASTERN ENTRANCE, APPROACHED BY A SUSPENSION BRIDGE ERECTED IN 1880

game hunters. There are gardening gloves and visiting-cards in the hall, the tradesmen come driving out from Kvaerndrup and Odense.

The rooms, as might be expected in a house which has survived four centuries and seems good for four more, represent most styles and periods of the past four hundred years. They range from the cellars, sternly utilitarian and designed to withstand a long siege, through panelled chambers to elegant eighteenth century salons.

Of course, Egeskov has its legends. In the roof of the stairway tower lies, to this day, a little wooden man. He is treated with some respect, for it is said that unless, on the night before Christmas Eve each year, he is given clean straw for his bed, the castle will sink into the lake. So seriously did the family take this threat in former times that Egeskov was always empty at Christmas.

But Egeskov has survived. In Kvaerndrup church is the tomb of Frands Brockenhuus, who built Egeskov, and of his wife, through whom he acquired it. The village churches of Europe are full of such memorials to the people who built and dwelt in the great houses under which they nestle. But too often those houses are empty now, or put to some excellent, if utilitarian, purpose which their builders never envisaged, and many of them have vanished altogether. Frands Brockenhuus and his heirs have been allowed to build on firm ground, and for that every discerning traveller in Denmark should be thankful.

Ewan Butler

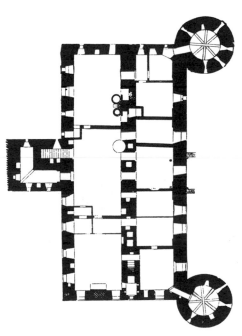

THE GROUND-PLAN OF THE ORIGINAL CASTLE

EGESKOV

ONE OF THE FARM BUILDINGS

below: IN THE HALL THE ROOF-BEAMS
WITH THEIR CARVED CORBELS ARE ORIGINAL

THE DINING-ROOM ON THE EAST SIDE

CAST-IRON STOVE IN THE PARLOUR

THE CELLARS UNDER THE WEST WING

A private house enclosed in a fortress

THE THICK WALLS PROVIDE CONVENIENT NICHES FOR GARDENING GLOVES
AND A TELEPHONE

AN ENGRAVING OF THE VILLA IN 1874

Villa Barbaro, Maser

Palladio's charming villa, embellished by Veronese

AS HE DRIVES EAST from Milan, or crosses the Adige from the south at Rovigo, the observant traveller is at once conscious of a change. All around him is evidence of ancient prosperity; country houses are more numerous; churches more imposing, their tall campaniles silhouetted against the foothills; gardens are filled with sculpture; even the villages are built with dignity and the soil itself seems more fruitful, its cultivation denser and more abundant. This is the legacy, more than a century and a half after its extinction, of the beneficent rule of the Venetian Republic. From the Lake of Garda to Friuli, villas are scattered across the Venetian plain, with a thick concentration along the Brenta: a density of architectural merit unequalled in any other countryside in the world. Among all of them, Villa Barbaro must rank as *primus inter pares*. It is the only one where we can admire the collaboration of two supreme geniuses, Palladio and Paolo Veronese; and thanks to good fortune and the care of successive owners, none is better preserved.

The most agreeable approach to Maser is from Padua. The road passes through a green luxuriance of vines, olives and maize, through the mediaeval walled town of Castelfranco, with a famous altar-piece by Giorgione in the church, and skirts the hill of Asolo crowned by Caterina Cornaro's palace. Maser is about two miles further along a country road. The Villa stands at the end of a straight gravel drive on the left of the road, seen through a railing flanked by stone figures of helmeted warriors, holding spear and shield. Jupiter, Juno and other statues line the gravel. The church, constructed in 1580 by Palladio as the Villa's chapel, is in front. On the right is a fountain with a figure of

VILLA BARBARO, MASER

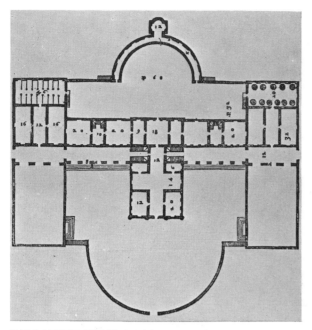

PALLADIO'S PLAN OF THE VILLA

Neptune and a long avenue of limes opposite the centre of the Villa. The façade is of two storeys, consisting of a central block, said to have been modelled on the Temple of Fortuna Virilis in Rome, with three pairs of windows between four engaged Ionic columns which support a frieze and pediment. Lower recessed arcaded wings on either side, with keystones carved with grotesque masks, were intended as granaries, store-houses, stables and agent's quarters for the estate. A shallow projection at each end supports a square surface adorned with a sun-dial, topped by a small pediment and flanked by curved buttresses. The low silhouette, to which the three pediments impart a lively movement, is strikingly in harmony with the dancing hills of the Grappa beyond. Constructed of brick faced with stucco, its whiteness as well as its architectural rhythm is emphasised by a plantation of trees behind. At the rear, the wings project to enclose a courtyard and the slope of the hill has been ingeniously used to reduce the height to a single storey, bringing the garden level with the *Piano Nobile*.

Daniele and Marcantonio Barbaro, for whom the Villa was built, belonged to one of the oldest, most distinguished and most

below: THE VILLA STANDS ON A SLIGHT RISE ABOVE THE PLAIN

cultivated families of Venice, which had held high office as early as the ninth century. They were born respectively in 1513 and 1518. Daniele inherited the family tendency to humanist scholarship. He performed the various duties expected of a young Venetian nobleman, culminating in his appointment as Ambassador to Edward VI of England from 1548 to 1550. Shortly after his return, he re-entered the Church and became Patriarch of Aquileia. Marcantonio was Ambassador to France from 1561 to 1564 and to Turkey from 1568 to 1574. There is no documentary confirmation of the date, but it seems now to be accepted that it was about 1560 that the brothers decided to build a villa on their estate at Maser. Although intended chiefly for the use of Marcantonio's family and descendants, as the senior branch, it is probable that Daniele, as the connoisseur of art, was the first originator of the idea; and the choice of architect and artist was certainly his, as well as of Alessandro Vittoria for the sculpture.

The *Piano Nobile* of the villa is divided into several relatively small rooms round a central cruciform hall, all with coved ceilings. On either side of this hall, on the main façade, are two rooms known as the *Sala di Bacco* (now the dining-room) and the *Sala degli Sposi*. At the garden-end the top of the cross has been divided off to form a square saloon, the *Aula*, from which a line of rooms extends to left and right along the garden. The walls and ceilings of all these rooms are decorated with frescoes by Paolo Veronese assisted by G. B. Zelotti and others. Painted at the height of his powers, when he was about thirty-two, this cycle of frescoes is not only the most important surviving record of his art, but must rank among the most beautiful domestic decorations ever created. In the central hall, which was originally open to the south, the frescoes have suffered and the landscapes are mostly modern restorations. Fortunately they seem to have been the work of assistants, and Veronese's own paintings in this room have survived. Only 'the festoons and leafy branches' on the ceiling, described by Cavalier Carlo Ridolfi in his life of Paolo Veronese published in 1646, have now disappeared. But elsewhere the frescoes are in excellent condition, and seem to have been painted with a special gusto.

Handsome large chimney-pieces in the *Sala di Bacco* and *degli Sposi* are the only architectural features inside the house, but the cycle of frescoes follows an architectural plan which harmonises perfectly with Palladio's conceptions. The walls are painted with Corinthian columns, landscapes seen through arches, gilt and marble statues in niches, more statues on pedimented overdoors; the scenes from myth and allegory, no doubt chosen by Daniele Barbaro, are mostly confined to the ceilings or overdoors. Each room is made to appear an open arcade looking over the countryside, an effect of depth and variety without which the cruciform hall, with only a single window, would scarcely have escaped a gloomy monotony. The landscapes are derived from the Venetian lagoons or the Grappa hills; innumerable details convey the summer riches of the mainland – no doubt the season when he was at work. A sense of abundance pervades the whole cycle. All the skies are blue; clouds appear only as a necessary support to the divinities of Olympus; even when Winter and Autumn are personified,

THE CHAPEL WAS BUILT BY PALLADIO IN 1580

THE COLONNADE OF THE WESTERN LOGGIA

THE 'NINFEO' GROTTO BEHIND THE HOUSE

91

VILLA BARBARO, MASER

THE CENTRAL HALL, WITH TWO FIGURES BY VERONESE

ANDREA PALLADIO (*left*), and PAOLO VERONESE,
FROM ENGRAVINGS BY GIOVANNI BATTISTA CECCHI

the sun shines on them; and the gods and goddesses themselves, humane, beautiful and glowing with health, are unmistakably Venetians. Religious subjects appear only in two of the bedrooms.

Around the *Aula* where the coved ceiling starts, is painted a balcony on which various members of the household stand. Marcantonio's wife, richly dressed, looks down at the visitor; an old nurse at her side glances across her at a small boy, the six-year old Alvise, her third son. On the parapet are perched a puppy and a parrot. On the opposite wall are the two elder sons: Francesco, aged fourteen, a studious boy clothed in black and reading a book; and twelve-year old Almoro, gaily dressed and fondling a hunting-dog, with a monkey on the parapet between them.

The final *trompe-l'œil* is reserved for the walls at either end of the suite of rooms along the garden. Both are painted with figures entering from outside. On the left the mistress of the house is depicted, flushed from the heat of the garden and fanning herself. From the other end a dapper young sportsman enters, with a shotgun and two hounds. The latter figure is traditionally identified as Veronese himself. If so, the artist's audacity in portraying himself for posterity in a position that belonged of right to Marcantonio Barbaro, is breathtaking.

The small garden, enclosed on three sides by the house, is partly turfed and partly paved with ornamental pebbles. On the fourth side, beyond a round pool, is the *Ninfeo*, a curved façade with stucco statues and ornament topped by a long low pediment supported by two youthful, and two mature, Atlases. In the centre an arched grotto contains a river god and a goddess pouring water into a pool. Five niches on either side hold classical figures, each with a satyrical aphorism in verse engraved below.

The Barbaros died out in the eighteenth century and Maser passed to the Basadona, then to the Manin, the family of the last Doge of Venice. The nineteenth century was a bad time for the Venetian aristocracy and for their villas, many of which were demolished or fell into decay. Villa Barbaro was lucky in passing into the possession of a rich industrialist, Giacomelli, who preserved it lovingly, though his restorations were in some instances ill-judged. It has been still more fortunate in the wise and tactful care, and the generous hospitality of its present owner, Contessa Marina Luling Buschetti Volpi.

Anthony Hobson

Veronese's frescoes are masterpieces of decoration

HIS VIVID COMBINATION OF CLASSICAL WITH DOMESTIC SUBJECTS

AULA, UPON WHICH MARCANTONIO'S WIFE LOOKS DOWN

right: THE FIGURE DESCRIBED AS VERONESE'S SELF-PORTRAIT

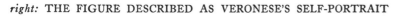

95

THE SITTING-ROOM, WITH A VIEW OF VERONESE'S 'SELF-PORTRAIT'

A BEDROOM, WITH A PORTRAIT OF MARCANTONIO'S WIFE

below: A CORNER OF THE AULA

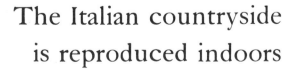

The Italian countryside
is reproduced indoors

osite: THE SALA DI BACCO, NOW THE DINING-ROOM

THE WEST FAÇADE, 'MORE GLASS THAN WALL'

Hardwick Hall

Elizabethan architecture at its most adventurous

ONE WRITER HAS CALLED HARDWICK HALL 'the most successful and best preserved of the great Palaces of the Elizabethan Renaissance'; another, 'the last and belated masterpiece of the Perpendicular'. Hardwick in fact is both, and its attraction is largely due to this bold blend of the classical and the late mediaeval.

Perpendicular Gothic, a manner native to Britain, was an ecclesiastical idiom, but at the very moment when the style produced its finest achievements, such as King's College Chapel at Cambridge, the building of great churches in England was ceasing. In such circumstances it was natural that many features of Perpendicular – a distaste for curves, an insistence on flat surfaces and rectilinear construction, and a love of walls that were largely glass – should find expression in domestic building. Thus at the end of the sixteenth century a number of imposing houses relate to Perpendicular, and for all their Renaissance decoration are as unlike Continental building as the style from which they derive.

Hardwick is the most notable example of such a house. The translation of at least one feature of Perpendicular is reflected at Hardwick in the popular adage, 'Hardwick Hall, more glass than wall'. The immense glazed areas of the façades at Hardwick were comparable, until the architecture of the twentieth century, only with the windows of late Perpendicular churches. Though houses such as

BUILDING ACCOUNTS, 1593, SIGNED
BY THE COUNTESS OF SHREWSBURY

ELIZABETH, COUNTESS OF SHREWSBURY

PORTRAIT OF ELIZABETH I AT HARDWICK

Wollaton, Wooton, and Doddington are related to Hardwick, the Perpendicular idiom was never achieved elsewhere in a country house with the same monumental effect or the same easy assurance.

The builder of Hardwick was as remarkable as the building. The Countess of Shrewsbury, familiarly known as Bess of Hardwick, was a squire's daughter who married four husbands, and so profited by the death of each that at last only the other Bess, the Queen of England, was richer. Her devotion to her second husband, Sir William Cavendish, does not obscure the fact that she was a tough scheming woman, but she earns her place in sixteenth-century history by the fact that she loved building as much as money. In addition to Hardwick, she built large houses at Chatsworth, Worksop, Oldcotes, and Bolsover. In 1590 the death of her fourth husband, Lord Shrewsbury, from whom she had been long estranged, made her mistress of vast additional resources. A month later, in her seventy-first year, she began the building of Hardwick, only a stone's throw away from an earlier mansion, now ruinous, where she had been born and to which she had already made ambitious additions.

Though his name does not occur among the accounts which have survived at Hardwick, Robert Smythson, associated with such great sixteenth-century houses as Longleat and Wollaton, was perhaps her architect. On the other hand, the formidable widow herself must almost certainly have dictated many of the features of the building. On her death she left Hardwick to her favourite son William, first Earl of Devonshire, and it thus passed into the powerful Cavendish family. This was providential. The Cavendishes owned vast estates and a number of great houses. Before the beginning of the eighteenth century Chatsworth had become their favoured Derbyshire seat, and consequently throughout the ensuing two hundred and fifty years Hardwick Hall suffered little transformation. Changes in fashion passed it by and it preserved, like a vast private warehouse, the taste and furnishings of Bess of Hardwick and the seventeenth-century Cavendishes who succeeded her. One of the least altered houses in England, both inside and out, it passed into the care of the National Trust in 1949.

Unlike most houses of its time Hardwick stands on a hill-top, and it dominates the Derbyshire countryside. The park with its aging stag-headed oaks climbs steeply to the gatehouse and the formal forecourt whose low walls are surmounted with a crenellation of strange pinnacles. Across the forecourt the house rises tier on tier. At sunset it is a shimmer of glass, the light reflected from thousands of diamond panes. Architecturally the impact of the building is largely due to the apparent contrast between vast areas of window, increasing in size with each storey, and a design which is notably compact. The house soars, yet sits as firmly as a tithe barn. The severe rectilinear effect of unnumbered mullions and transoms is wonderfully set off by the fretted cresting of the roof-line, where the initials ES (for Elizabeth Shrewsbury) appear among coronets and dancing scrolls. At ground level the two salient towers of the south façade are linked by a sturdy Tuscan loggia, the most striking classical element in this

Perpendicular design.

Though Hardwick incorporates the features common to most fine Elizabethan houses – hall, Long Gallery, and Great Chamber – each at Hardwick is in its own way unusual. The hall is perhaps the first in England to be treated simply as an entrance hall, and its axis runs, counter to mediaeval precedent, transversely from the front of the house to the back, though the conception of the usual hall 'screens' is retained in a fine screen of Tuscan columns. Over the fireplace is an enormous heraldic cartouche with elaborate strapwork, incorporating Bess of Hardwick's arms. It is a notable example of those plaster overmantels and friezes for which Hardwick is renowned. Flemish in derivation, but largely the work of an English plasterer, Abraham Smith, they have a boldness, a simplicity, and a poetry that are native. In the hall are also many examples of the Hardwick collection of needlework and tapestry, a collection probably unparalleled in any private house in Europe. The most unusual, and beautiful, of the needlework panels are the astonishing representations of the Virtues at the east end of the hall. Applied 'on cloth of golde velvett and other like stuff', they are really a type of *collage*. The needlework throughout the house is largely contemporary with Bess of Hardwick, and some of it, not without reason, has been attributed to Mary Queen of Scots. Though she was never confined at Hardwick, Lord Shrewsbury (the Countess's fourth husband) was the queen's goaler for fifteen years.

SOUTH WING. 'E S' ARE THE COUNTESS' INITIALS

The Long Gallery, a peculiarly English development, runs at Hardwick the whole length of the east front. In size it is second only to the gallery at Montacute in Somerset, and its walls are covered with the thirteen Brussels tapestries, depicting the story of Gideon, which Bess of Hardwick bought in 1592. Against these tapestries are hung, and apparently have been so hung for generations, portraits of Queen Elizabeth and Mary Queen of Scots, of successive Cavendishes, and of figures associated with the long history of the house.

The Great Chamber, next to the Long Gallery, is in Sacheverell Sitwell's opinion 'the most beautiful room, not in England alone, but in the whole of Europe'. With its contemporary plasterwork, tapestries, and furniture, it is certainly one of the most homogeneous and untouched, and it perhaps expresses most finely the sense of contact with the past that Hardwick repeatedly conveys. On the deep plaster frieze, now muted in colour but with a poetry that is unfading, the chase proceeds under green trees and Diana holds her court. Beneath the frieze the story of Ulysses is told in a set of Brussels tapestries which the Countess bought two years before she started building. The marble fireplace, while incorporating the strapwork characteristic of the period, is like others at Hardwick of a splendid restraint and comparable in this respect to the great fireplaces at Bramshill in Hampshire. The tables and sideboards of elaborate design, deriving from Franco-Flemish prototypes, occur as does much of the other furniture at Hardwick in an inventory of 1601, and the farthingale chairs are covered with an original sixteenth-century needlework. By contrast a set of rich Charles II stools seems almost a modern importa-

THE CONCLVSION OF ALL THINGS IS TO FEARE GOD AND KEEPE HIS COMMAVNDEMENTES

15 S 97

OVERMANTEL OF THE DINING-ROOM FIREPLACE

THE WALLED ELIZABETHAN GARDEN

tion. On the floor is rush matting of the particular weave that has always been used at Hardwick, and that has come to be known elsewhere as 'Hardwick matting'.

Authenticity is the note struck. There are houses more elegant, possibly more beautiful, but the impression of a great house as it must have looked and felt in the late sixteenth and seventeenth centuries is surely nowhere else so immediate. Room after room, with its plaster decoration, its panelling or its tapestried walls that muffle sound, its furniture that seems never to have been moved, remains after four hundred years complete and convincing. Hardwick is a house with an almost oppressive feeling of time and, for all its great windows, a house of shadows.

Even the garden at Hardwick has retained, like Chastleton in Gloucestershire and a few other houses, its early formal character and escaped 'improvement' in the eighteenth century. Between yew hedges and down the alleys of pleached fruit trees such as still exist, the Countess might well have walked. Bacon himself might have approved the lay-out.

Robin Fedden

THE QUEEN OF SCOTS BEDROOM
left: STONE STAIRCASE TO THE UPPER FLOORS

opposite: BEDHEAD TAPESTRY IN THE STATE BED-CHAMBE

ENTRANCE TO THE GREAT HIGH CHAMBER

Hardwick remains almost unaltered

'SUMMER', DETAIL OF PLASTER-WORK

HAM SMITH

THE FIREPLACE OF THE GREAT HIGH CHAMBER

left: A PLASTER FRIEZE OF DIANA WITH HER HUNTRESSES

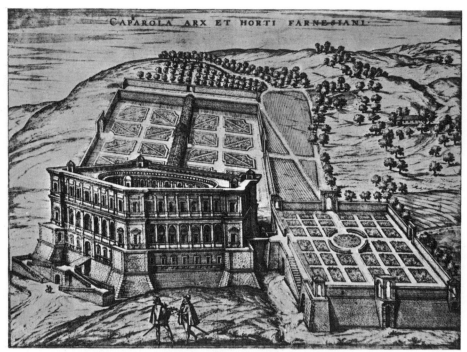

Caprarola

Vignola's masterpiece in the Monti Cimini

THE MONTI CIMINI, a range of thickly wooded volcanic hills, lie thirty-five miles to the north-west of Rome. After travelling through the woods over empty country roads, past the Lake of Vico, one reaches a gorge down which rushes a noisy torrent. On the far bank, the modest village of Caprarola is built on the hillside, its grey stone houses merging into the background. At the top of the hill stands the vast bulk of the Farnese Palace, reddish gold in the sunlight, dominating the village like a lion. The contrast between Caprarola's towering Renaissance architecture and the wildness of its surroundings is unique in its dramatic impact.

Cardinal Alessandro Farnese, who built Caprarola, is familiar from Titian's portrait of him with his grandfather, the aged Pope Paul III, at Naples. But this painting, which has come to be considered the classic portrayal of Papal nepotism, does not do justice to the Cardinal's own qualities. Contemporaries are agreed on his generosity, his courteous manners, the dignity of his presence and his patronage of artists and men-of-letters. In 1550, however, the Cardinal's fortunes were at their lowest. It was the policy of Pope Julius III to bring down the Farnese from the commanding position they had attained in the previous reign. Cardinal Alessandro decided that it would be advisable to retire for a time from Rome. His choice of Caprarola as the place for his retreat was determined by various considerations;

106

opposite: VIGNOLA'S ASTONISHING SPIRAL STAIRCASE

CAPRAROLA

THE DOUBLE STAIRWAY OF THE ENTRANCE

THE ENTRANCE FAÇADE

A GROTESQUE
WATER MASK

THE CATENA D'ACQUA FLOWS FROM THE LOGGIA

THE SCALA REGIA RISES THREE STOREY

A ROW OF HUGE STONE
CANEPHORAE ENCIRCLES THE
PARTERRE OF THE CASINO

A fortress softened
by the humanism
of the Renaissance

108

it lay in the Farnese fief of Ronciglione; it was neither too near nor too far from the capital; and the wildness of the country both guaranteed warning against any surprise, and, it may be, harmonised with the apparent ruin of his ambitions. The Bolognese architect Vignola, who had felt the powerful influence of Michelangelo while in Rome, was commissioned to plan a suitable villa and started work in March 1550.

The site was already chosen for him, the remains of an early fortress, a *Rocca*, that had crowned the hill. The building is pentagonal in shape and stands on a platform supported by five bastions at the corners. It is surrounded by a narrow moat crossed by three drawbridges, one on the façade, the other leading to the garden at the back. The architecture is severe, decorated only with pilasters and pedimented windows, alternately round and triangular, somewhat recalling the Escorial in its austerity. An extra storey, the *Sotterranei*, was excavated out of the tufa below the foundations.

An ingenious series of stairs and terraces joins the village to the palace. From a piazza at the top of the village a double flight of steps leads to a large rectangular terrace, used for the manœuvres of the Cardinal's cavalry, supported on three rusticated arches. From here another balustraded double-staircase, on either side of the arched entrance to the *Sotterranei*, a warren of kitchens and store-rooms, rises to the main entrance. This is again a rusticated arch, set between six windows in the front of the platform, and giving access to the ground floor, the *Piano dei Prelati*.

The centre of the building contains a circular arcaded courtyard, supporting, on the level of the *Piano Nobile*, a balustraded gallery with Ionic columns arranged in pairs around niches which are said once to have held busts of Roman Emperors. A magnificent circular staircase, the *Scala Regia*, in the left angle of the façade, leads from the ground floor to the higher storeys. Superbly proportioned, it is carried on pairs of columns the sight of which, it is related, provoked Cardinal Alessandro to seize Vignola's hand and call him 'a second Vitruvius'. Walls and ceiling are frescoed with arabesques, allegories and symbolic devices by Antonio Tempesta. The twelve staterooms on the *Piano Nobile* are notable for their frescoes by the Zuccaro brothers. The subjects of the paintings, down to the smallest detail of composition and figures, were laid down by Annibale Caro, the Cardinal's secretary; the specifications for a single room occupy eighteen printed pages in Vasari. The deeds of the Farnese family were naturally prominent among the subjects; Alexander the Great is introduced in compliment to the Cardinal; Hercules figures because as a child he was nursed by the goat Amaltheia, a punning reference to Caprarola thoroughly typical of humanist thought.

The lower garden is reached by a drawbridge from behind the *Piano Nobile*. It is of the usual formal type, box parterres with fountains, statues and grottoes, now much decayed and lacking the unique inspiration of Villa Lante. One grotto, hung with stalactites and supported by huge stucco fauns, was used in the seventeenth century as a theatre and witnessed many performances of Guarini's colourless

GALLERY OF THE CIRCULAR COURTYARD

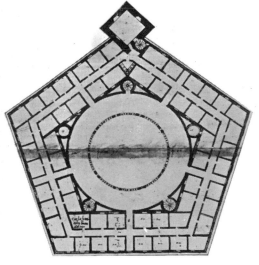

VIGNOLA'S ORIGINAL DRAWING OF THE GROUND-PLAN

drama *Il Pastor Fido*. From the lower garden one ascends through oak-woods to arrive, across a lawn, at an open space with a fountain. From here an elaborate architectural composition rises to the celebrated casino, one of the most admired features of Caprarola, constructed after Cardinal Alessandro's death by Cardinal Odoardo Farnese. Two sets of rusticated arches enclose a ramp, divided by a *catena d'acqua* (similar to the one at Villa Lante) which flows from a grotto surmounted by two gigantic river-gods. The casino has an arcaded loggia, frescoed with arabesques, and a tiled roof. Around it is another parterre, on the summit of the hill, with box-hedges and fountains, surrounded by a low wall supporting a row of huge *Canephorae*, stone terms carrying baskets on their heads.

Caprarola is even more empty and desolate than the country in which it so incongruously stands, and an effort is needed to imagine the activity that filled it at the time of its completion. On the lower terraces and along the balustrades would have been the Cardinal's guards, in uniforms powdered with the Farnese lilies. Horsemen wheeled and galloped outside the entrance to the *Sotterranei*, while inside the latter all was hectic with hurrying cooks, butlers and cellarers. On the *Piano dei Prelati* were the guardroom, Annibale Caro's rooms and office, no doubt also the rooms for the Cardinal's distinguished guests. But the centre of the household was on the *Piano Nobile*, where groups of gentlemen-in-waiting, chaplains, prelates, petitioners – even sightseers like Montaigne – collected or made way before the Cardinal and his intimates.

Cardinal Alessandro died in 1589, leaving Caprarola to his family again, reigning in the Duchy of Parma, and more particularly for the use of any future Farnese Cardinal. A visit by the Old Pretender in the following century was perhaps the final flicker of Caprarola's brilliance, for in 1731 the last Farnese Duke of Parma died and the family's property passed to the Spanish, and thence to the Neapolitan, Bourbons. The Farnese collections and library were removed to Naples and the villa entered a long period of neglect. After the unification of Italy it was lived in by the Count of Caserta, younger son of King Ferdinando, in circumstances of mounting decay, and has only recently been acquired by the Italian state. The casino in the upper garden is now reserved for the Italian President and a special permit is needed to visit it.

If the first impression of Caprarola is amazement at its size and wild surroundings, and the second of admiration at Vignola's resolution of the peculiar difficulties of the site, this should not blind us to the real beauties of its architecture. It is the finest achievement in a landscape setting of the Italian Renaissance school, based on the principles of Vitruvius, which strove to use ornament with the utmost economy, to avoid the merely decorative and to achieve the harmony of ideal proportion.

Anthony Hobson

THE HALL OF THE FARNESE ANNALS, DECORATED BY THE
ZUCCARO BROTHERS WITH SCENES FROM THE HISTORY
OF THE FAMILY. A PORTRAIT OF PHILIP II IS ABOVE THE
CENTRAL DOOR

PARIS IN THE SEVENTEENTH CENTURY. HÔTEL LAMBERT MARKED 'F'

Hôtel Lambert,

A President's house on an island in the Seine

Paris semble à mes yeux un pays de roman,
J'y croyais ce matin voir une île enchantée
Je la laissai déserte et la trouve habitée...

CORNEILLE, STRUCK BY the oddness of the sudden transformation, saluted with these verses in *Le Menteur* the expansion of the Île Saint-Louis, twin island to the Cité; in the heart of Paris, yet how different in aspect, history and customs. Up to the reign of Henri IV, it had been waste land visited only by strolling players and archers; washerwomen landed from boats to spread out their linen, and cows browsed in green pastures. In less than thirty years, it was to assume its present-day aspect. The Pont Neuf having been thrown across from the other side of the Cité, a contractor was tempted to take advantage of this space belonging to the Chapter of Notre Dame. Between 1630 and 1650, the quays were paved, the bridges finished, the roads outlined, all these being at right angles to the back-bone of the island. Jean-Baptiste Lambert, lord of Sucy and of Thorigny, Secretary to the King, bought the portions which, joined together, serve as a base for the superb Hôtel Lambert.

Louis Levau worked there for two years – probably with d'Orbais, as is now suggested – and was so taken with the site that he built a modest medium-sized dwelling for himself. At Easter 1644, Jean-Baptiste Lambert installed himself there; for a short time only, since he was to die on the 22nd December at the age of 36. Jean-Baptiste's heir was his brother Nicolas, who in 1671 became President of the Chambre des Comptes. In the reign of the Great King, Nicolas Lam-

BRONZE RELIEF BY VAN OBSTAL

bert enjoyed a fortune estimated at more than 3,000,000 livres. He was implicated in the Foucquet trial, was taxed at a million livres, and saw his fourteen estates seized and put up for sale. He paid the enormous tax, however, remained a landowner, and in 1685 married his eldest son Claude to the daughter of Alexander Bontemps, the all-powerful First Valet de Chambre of Louis XIV.

The three artists engaged on the house were Levau, Lesueur and Le Brun. Blondel's engravings allow us to hover over each storey in its original condition. Entering by the Rue Saint- Louis, we penetrate into the main courtyard: on the right are the kitchens, the servants' hall, and, under the great gallery, the stables; on the left, the coach-houses and the fruit loft; on each side of the flight of steps, the wine-cellars. The first floor at the height of the steps is on a level with the garden ornamented with flower beds. Anterooms precede the library, underneath the gallery.

The ceremonial floor amazes us after its recent restoration. We mount by the great staircase, whose two flights of stairs wind on each side of an arched semi-dome, decorated in black and white with a river-god and a naiad, attributed to Eustache Lesueur. The steps bring us majestically to the oval vestibule decorated with bas-reliefs in black and white after Lesueur. Going straight through between two Corinthian columns we enter the gallery of *The Apotheosis of Hercules,* 'which', says Blondel, 'is one of the most beautiful works of Charles Le Brun'.

It is the first monumental work of the great scene-painter who later embellished Vaux-le-Vicomte, Versailles, the Louvre and Sceaux. Five windows look out onto the garden, opposite recesses decorated with landscapes as in the Mazarin Gallery of the present Bibliothèque Nationale, the sister building of 1645. Three windows looking

LEVAU'S GALERIE D'HERCULE DECORATED BY LE BRUN

THE FAÇADE FROM THE PONT SULLY

ENTRANCE FROM THE COUR D'HONNEUR

PRESIDENT LAMBERT DE THORIGNY

over the Seine open in a terminal half-circle slightly reminiscent of the poop of a ship-of-the-line. Between the casements and the recesses, are alternate octagonal and oval medallions in bronze stucco by Van Obstal, dedicated to the exploits of Hercules and supported in graceful fashion by Cupids, sad-faced Sphinxes, spreading Eagles and busts of the god Terminus. The richness of the decoration is not detrimental to the grace of the whole. This alliance of Italian grandeur and of French moderation is a Parisian miracle that still moves all visitors.

Three resplendent rooms, antechambers or salons, open upon the oval vestibule. One of them, called the Room of the Muses, is painted by Lesueur with a variety of subjects: on the ceiling, *Apollo lending his chariot to Phaeton*; on the circumference, *The Nine Muses*. In a closet, says Argenville, 'Lesueur painted the Moon in her chariot in the form of Diana, preceded by Lucifer, who marks the dawn'. This is an original painting which has been preserved in the mansion in the form of a picture. Everywhere, gilded wainscotting, decorated with arabesques, with garlands of flowers and medallions supported by Cupids, gives the final touch in according to the reception room that sumptuous character which makes it the undoubted offspring of the Galerie Farnèse.

Lambert, who was surnamed 'Lambert the Rich', was enjoying the unequalled splendour of his Parisian mansion when he died on the 8th May, 1692. His son Claude only kept it for a period of ten years and, departing this life in 1702, passed on his inheritance to his younger brother Nicolas-Louis, President of the Parlement, who died a bachelor in 1729.

In 1739, Florent-Claude, Marquis du Châtelet, and his wife, Emilie de Breteuil, bought the building for 180,000 livres. To speak of Emilie is to introduce Voltaire. In 1742, he was already lodging in a little room on the upper floor. The inexhaustible letter-writer gives us his opinion of the place: 'Mme du Châtelet has just bought a house made for a philosopher monarch. It is happily in a neighbourhood far from everything: which is how it has come about that they have had for 200,000 francs what cost two millions to build and ornament'. The beautiful Emilie's fancy for the author of *Candide* lasted much longer than that she had conceived for the Hôtel Lambert. As early as 1744, it was let to the Portuguese ambassador, and the following year it was sold at a loss of 20,000 francs to the tax-farmer Marin de la Haye. Cold and unpleasing, yet a fervent art lover, Marin de la Haye died childless in 1753. His widow, Marie-Edmée de Saint-Marc, occupied his residence until her own death in 1776. Nephews and nieces then hastened to disperse the collection and the mansion's treasures.

In 1781, a Davesne de Fontaine, Correcteur aux Comptes, was the owner of the impoverished building, and in 1809, the Comte de Montalivet, Minister of the Interior, installed himself there. It appears that he decorated his château of Berry with painted panels surviving from the previous dismemberment. What could have been the state of the house during the Restoration, in its humble functions of a boarding school for young girls and then of a storehouse for military beds?

Banished from Poland in 1831, after one of the Polish insurrections against the Russians, Prince Adam Czartoryski took refuge in France. In May 1842, Princess Czartoryska contended with the city of Paris for the Hôtel Lambert, where they wished to install their Library, and she obtained it by bidding 5,000 francs more than the 175,000 offered by the municipality. During the second half of the nineteenth century, the Hôtel Lambert was the capital of the Polish province into which the île Saint-Louis had been transformed. The heirs of Prince Adam Czartoryski have recently permitted Baron de Redé to take charge of an elegant restoration of the reception floor, which in the Great Century was the admiration of connoisseurs. The painted panels wrested from the Room of the Muses have been replaced by reputable paintings which best suit the sumptuous frames. Rare furnishings, emblazoned books, silverware, bronzes of peerless elegance, animate with their presence the magnificent apartments resurrected after a sleep longer than that of the Sleeping Beauty.

René Héron de Villefosse

THE GALERIE D'HERCULE IN 1740

THE SALLE D'AMOUR. ENGRAVINGS BY PICARD

CHARLES LE BRUN, LOUIS XIV'S COURT PAINTER

Few houses have recovered so splendidl

LOOKING BACK FROM THE GALERIE D'HERCULE

THE OVAL VESTIBULE LEADS INTO

ORMOLU DECORATION ON A LOUIS XVI CABINET

rom a temporary decline

LLERY

THE LIBRARY

ENGRAVING OF THE GARDEN FRONT BY ISRAEL SYLVESTRE

Château de Tanlay

A splendid union of stone and clear water

VISITORS TO THE CHÂTEAU de Tanlay turn into an avenue of two-hundred-year-old limes. As the lime-trees finish, they find themselves in a broad village street, a few houses on each side, a church on the right, a gateway in front and beyond it, a doll's-house château, the Petit Château de Tanlay, with dummy windows and elaborate rustication. Passing through the arch in its centre, they enter a huge court-yard. To the right, a similar wall hides the older – and in itself very beautiful – farmyard court. To the left is at last revealed the moat, the obelisks which flank the bridge, the gate-house and the château.

Tanlay, except for minor changes to the wings, remains as conceived by its owner at the time of its building, Michel de Particelli, and as realised by his architect, Pierre Le Muet, who used as a basis the old fortified castle of the Coligny d'Andelot family with its rectangular layout and its round towers at the corners. Michel de Particelli, *Intendant et Contrôleur Général des Finances*, bought Tanlay from the Coligny d'Andelot family in 1642 and set Le Muet to work the following year. The reconstruction was finished in 1648. Particelli had the vast fortune which the project required, and Le Muet had the genius for turning Particelli's money into a great work of art. After Particelli's death, the property passed, through his sister, to Jehan Thévenin, *Conseilleur du Roi*, Governor of Saint-Denis, Marquis de Tanlay, and has remained in the Tanlay family since 1704. The last marquis died five years ago and the château now belongs to his daughter, the Comtesse de la Chauvinière.

The château is built of warm, yellowish stone, the roof of slate-covered tiles, the domes having a shiny smoothness which looks almost

opposite: THE BRIDGE AND THE GATE-HOUSE

metallic. The garden side of Tanlay is even more elaborate than the courtyard side. Between the lanterned corner towers, ingeniously incorporated by Le Muet into his design, are two rows of almost severely simple windows. But simplicity turns to fantasy at roof level as Le Muet alternates his *œil-de-bœuf* dormer windows with triangle-topped oblong ones, all elaborately carved, giving the building a gaiety as well as an elegance that makes the visitor gasp with amazement.

Tanlay is surrounded by a moat twenty-one metres wide, profuse with yellow water-lilies and ancient carp. It does not have the usual look of moats, stagnant, slimy, full of algae and weeds, because it is supplied with fresh water. Particelli's project included bringing fresh water from the Cistercian Abbaye de Quincy about two miles away. The canal – at rather a strange angle from the château – is not only functional but is a feature of Particelli's landscaping of the château's surroundings. One looks along it and sees, half a mile away, a decorative wall of pillars and niches, which the French call a *château-d'eau*.

Tanlay has as many rewards within as without. The entrance is in the courtyard front. One enters a dead white hall, richly antlered, leading into the pillared *Vestibule des Césars*, white again, a room of extreme classical simplicity, its only decoration the busts of eight Caesars in niches in the wall. These two rooms are the width of the château and give a sense both of its strength and of its size. Historically, the most interesting room is on the top floor of one of the towers, La Tour de la Ligue. There Admiral Coligny and his brothers, all ardent Protestants, used to meet. The fresco on the ceiling represents the court of Charles IX, dressed – and undressed – as mythological characters: Admiral Coligny is, appropriately, Neptune; Diane de Poitiers, Venus; Catherine de Medici, Juno.

Architecturally, the most curious room is the gallery on the first floor, decorated entirely – walls and vaulted ceiling – in grey and white *trompe-l'œil*. Several of the rooms contain chimney-pieces from the

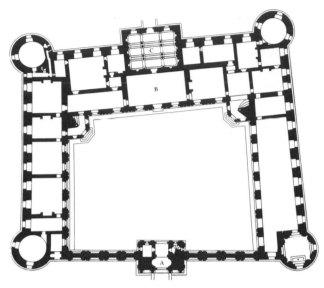

THE GROUND-FLOOR PLAN, WITH (A) THE GATE-HOUSE (B) THE HALL, (C) THE VESTIBULE DES CÉSARS

THE GARDEN FRONT FROM THE NORTH-WEST TURRET
right: THE DOME REFLECTED IN THE MOAT

Coligny days, fine examples of Louis XIII before the refinement and simplification of taste under Louis XVI. The furniture, which is superb, is the accumulation of generations of the Tanlay family: Louis XIV, Régence, Louis XV, Louis XVI. There are eighteenth-century Savonnerie carpets on the floor, eighteenth-century curtains are still hanging, and all the bedspreads and bed hangings are of that period. There are some fine chandeliers and, among many other *objets d'art*, a remarkable collection of *Compagnie des Indes* porcelain. Everywhere the arrangement has a perfection of charm and good taste. The chapel – in another of the towers – has two *prie-Dieux*, *signé* Jacob, for M. le Comte and Mme la Comtesse. The pictures are interesting both historically and aesthetically: Nattier, Largillière, Mignard, for example, painted members of the family.

The house and contents survived the Revolution. The Tanlays were not absentee landlords and the local peasantry had nothing against them. Although the Marquis and Marquise spent from December 1793 to October 1794 under arrest, during this time the house and its contents remained intact.

Robin McDouall

THE CHÂTEAU D'EAU, BY C. SAUVAGEAT

THE MOAT, GATE-HOUSE AND COUR D'HONNEUR

THE GARDEN FAÇADE WITH ITS LANTERNED CORNER TOWERS

below: THE RUSTICATION ON THE PETIT CHÂTEAU

One of the most
attractive châteaux
in France

A CORNER OF THE MAIN SALON

THE QUEEN'S BEDROOM

THE GREAT GALLERY, DECORATED THROUGHOUT IN TROMPE-L'ŒIL

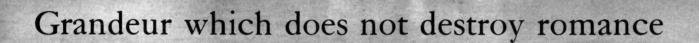

Isola Bella

Grandeur which does not destroy romance

ISOLA BELLA

THE COAT-OF-ARMS OF THE BORROMEOS

THE BALLROOM

ISOLA BELLA – the very words hold the sound of lapping water, capturing our imagination, evoking the memory of our first glimpse of Italy seen from the windows of a train. The great baroque building with its gardens hanging in terraces of oranges and myrtle above the blue waters of Maggiore appears as a symbol rather than a house.

In the seventeenth century, when nearly all Italy lay under Spanish domination, the Borromeos were already among the most powerful families of Lombardy and Piedmont. Their strongholds controlled the greater part of the Ticino and to the glory of their family scutcheon was added the saintly halo of San Carlo Borromeo. But for all their saints and cardinals, legend claims the Borromeos to have been descended from pirates. And perhaps it was in memory of his pirate forefathers that Vitaliano Borromeo, great-nephew to the saint, cousin to a cardinal, conceived his palace as a floating galleon anchored to a stony island with a garden shaped like the prow of a ship suspended above the water.

It was a bold conception, and the leading architects and engineers of Italy were consulted on the plans. Morelli presented the first designs, Barca laid out the gardens, but nothing would satisfy Vitaliano Borromeo until Fontana, the great architect of papal Rome, was enlisted in his service to design a palace on so vast a scale that both owner and architect died long before it was completed.

Seventy families live on the Borromean islands, families who for centuries have married among themselves and look upon the great house as a part of their heritage, while the attitude of a Borromeo towards the local inhabitants is rather that of a captain of a ship towards his crew – they are all part of a single unit, and no large party is ever given at the palace without the islanders being invited. From the custodian to the woman selling her laces on the quay, from the boatman plying between the island and the mainland to the padrone welcoming guests to his trattoria, everyone has an interest at stake in the house which is bringing in such handsome dividends. It is not only the local inhabitants who have grown rich on the tourists. Now at last after three hundred years the Isola Bella has been finally completed. When he declared that all money collected at the gates would be spent on keeping up the house, Prince Borromeo can never have imagined that within the first few years, there would be sufficient money not only to restore, but to finish the palace on the plans left by Fontana. It is a labour of love to which the humblest visitor paying his modest entrance fee can feel he has contributed. The great hectagonal building which rises three storeys high above the water is now balanced and harmonious, the cupola in the newly completed vaulted hall soars with the same aerial grace as Fontana's cupolas in Rome. The wood and plaster carvings with the ever-recurring motif of twisted ribbon, a motif one finds in other Borromean villas, is in the best baroque tradition. But even in its full glory, the Isola Bella, like any large flamboyant woman, depends on its setting and its dress to give the illusion of beauty.

The sunlit waters, the flowering gardens where camellias follow mimosas and azaleas follow camellias, the terraces sheltered by hedges of cypress and of yew, decorated with obelisks and statues, the cascading fountains and pavements inlaid with mosaic, are the accessories which enhance its charm, a charm which despite its grandeur remains essentially romantic, the setting for the idylls of Fogazzaro, the background for the canvasses of Turner and Corot.

Romantic and theatrical at the same time, for one never lands on Isola Bella without feeling one is taking part in the first act of a play. The gay holiday crowds coming off the boat, the brightly coloured stalls which line the island's only street, the hawkers displaying their wares in a shrill chorus, the women singing as they wash their linen in the lake, are all part of the overture which culminates in the dramatic ascent up the granite staircase to the house.

On entering, the first impact is somewhat of a shock: it is only now we realise we are in a seventeenth-century palace rather than a villa, a palace designed for viceroys and cardinals rather than for country gentlemen. From a hall sculptured with family coats of arms, decorated with weapons, we pass into the throne room, where three centuries ago a Borromeo dispensed justice in the name of a foreign king and Hapsburgs, Bourbons and Buonapartes have all in turn held court. The throne room leads to a library, the library to a ballroom and a somewhat disappointing picture gallery. Here in this alcoved bedroom, Napoleon slept after the treaty of Campo Formio had made him master of Italy. Napoleon paid two visits to the Isola Bella: the first time he came as a victorious general, driving over from his headquarters at Mombello; the second time he came as Emperor of the French accompanied by Josephine and a large retinue of generals and of courtiers. The Borromeos, who had had their stronghold of Angera destroyed by French troops, can hardly have been enthusiastic over entertaining the conqueror, but the *fête champêtre* they gave in his honour, at which Grassini the leading diva of the Scala sang his favourite arias, was on so magnificent a scale, as to earn Napoleon's thanks and gratitude.

Napoleon, and after him Mussolini – men whose over life-size personalities and love of dramatic gestures fit into these gilded mirrored rooms. Here in the so-called music room Mussolini presided over the Stresa Conference when he promised peace in Europe and no-one stopped to question his intentions overseas. Then just as we begin to pall of these pompous state apartments, we come upon one small unpretentious room decorated by Zucharelli with pastoral scenes of the various Borromean properties, Arona, Senago, and the rock of Angera. Light and delicate in conception, with an almost bucolic charm, this little room introduces a human note in the somewhat arid splendour of the Borromean palace, as if the artist had wished to remind the cardinals and statesmen of the simple pleasures which lay outside their gates. And we in turn are tempted to leave the palace by the long gallery hung with Flemish tapestries which leads into the gardens. For it is only in the gardens that we will find the answer to the legend of the Borromean islands, a legend fostered by generations of poets, treasured by generations of romantics.

Alexandre Dumas declared that the view of Isola Bella seen from

CEILING OF THE LONG GALLERY

WOOD AND PLASTER MOTIFS OF TWISTED RIBBON

PIGEONS SETTLE ON A STONE UNICORN

the mainland was so entrancing that it distracted him from working and that the articles he wrote while on holiday at Baveno were among the worst he had ever published. But what Dumas found distracting helped to soothe a greater and more tormented genius. On the terraces of the Isola Bella Richard Wagner re-found the peace of mind he had lost after his sudden flight from Zurich and the emotional turmoil of the Wesendonck menage.

Writing to Mathilde Wesendonck from Venice, he described his excursion to the Isola Bella: 'As I already knew the place, I dismissed the gardener in order to be alone. It was a lovely summer day and all of a sudden I felt serene and at peace. It was a feeling so marvellous that I knew it could not last. But what can last and what has become a part of me is our love and my need of you'.

At the time of writing, *Tristan* was barely completed, *Parsifal* was still in embryo, and one is tempted to wonder whether Kundry's enchanted garden was inspired by Wagner's memories of the Borromean islands, of those flower-laden terraces rising tier upon tier above the water, linked by a chain of fountains, with obelisks placed like masts guiding the course of a ship and the water dripping in the fountain basins echoing the murmur of the waves lapping against the shores of the Isola Bella.

Joan Haslip

THE PEACOCKS ARE AS ORNAMENTAL AS THE STATUES

ISOLA BELLA

AN EIGHTEENTH-CENTURY ENGRAVING   TURNER'S IDEALISATION OF THE SCENE
below: THE GARDENS LAID OUT BY BARCA ABOVE A SMALL LANDING STAGE

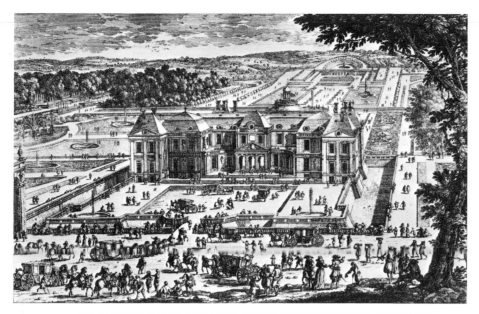

THE ENTRANCE FRONT IN THE LATE SEVENTEENTH CENTURY

Vaux-le-Vicomte

The most splendid house and garden in all France

THE PARK AND CHÂTEAU of Vaux-le-Vicomte, in their perfection, their purity and their unity, are linked in one's mind with the idea of youth. They represent a first perfect bloom unfolding at the dawn of the Great Century. Nevertheless it was the work of men who were already of mature years and in full possession of their powers. If its creators appear to be still marked by Italian influence, this is because Italy was very much the fashion, and not because their talent had not come to maturity.

Nicolas Foucquet bought the land of Vaux-le-Vicomte in 1641 at the age of 26. But he waited fifteen years before undertaking the building of the magnificent house, in which he flattered himself that he would live sumptuously for many years, surrounded by artists, writers, and beautiful women. So it was only in 1656 that the work began. Foucquet was 41, Levau 44, Le Nôtre 43, Le Brun 37. The 'Benjamin' of the team was, at 28, Girardon, and the oldest Nicolas Poussin, who at 62 doubtless appeared venerable in comparison.

They were a group of remarkable men. Nicolas Foucquet, one of those financial wizards whose daring methods fill the state coffers at critical moments, but whose fortune provokes the envious and the jurists to plan their ruin; Poussin, master of a school of painting so radiant that artists of the abstract still use its name, and whose work was not without influence on William Kent, Chambers, and the pioneers of landscape gardening; Le Brun, later first painter at the Court; Girardon, the elegant sculptor of goddesses in ethereal draperies; Le

VAUX-LE-VICOMTE

THE CUPOLA DATES FROM 1658

A MOAT AS WIDE AS A RIVER

TH

LAGES WERE REMOVED TO CREATE THIS VISTA

GIRARDON'S STATUES STAND
AGAINST WATER AND HEDGES

Nôtre, greatest of all the gardeners of France; finally, the architect, Louis Levau.

But of all the people involved in the history of Vaux, the youngest was the King. Louis XIV was 18 in 1656, and 23 in 1661, the year of the drama. He had always lived under the tutelage of Mazarin, and his childhood had not been very happy. The Cardinal's luxury no doubt had often infuriated him; it is said that he himself lacked fresh linen and clean sheets. It was easy for him to compare his own relative destitution and his tumble-down châteaux with the splendid edifice complete with all modern improvements, built by the Superintendent of Finance.

Through the hands of the latter passed the taxes levied on the people. It was certainly the custom to remunerate high officials with percentages of the money gathered. Did Foucquet take too much advantage of this, or did he conform to the generally accepted usage of his time? This was the whole crux of the trial which was to be his undoing. For a long time, his relations with Mazarin and Colbert had been stormy. Alarming reports, of whose gravity he was not unaware, had been rained upon him by his numerous informants; but he was reassured by his knowledge of the immense services for which the Queen Mother and the Cardinal were indebted to him. The thought that the ostentatious display of his wealth might be ill-advised did not cross his mid.

The work at Vaux-le-Vicomte progressed:

1656: Three villages were demolished to free the necessary space.
1657: The stonework was finished, marble-cutters laid the pavements and carpenters the panelling.
1658: The lantern was set upon the cupola.
1660: The ceilings were decorated, and during this time Le Nôtre laid the flower-beds and excavated sites for the sheets of water.

In 1661 Foucquet chose to receive in great pomp the young sovereign who was young enough to be his son. He interrupted the work to prepare the most dazzling fête ever known. All the Superintendent's household took part in it. There were fountain displays, illuminations, and performances of *Les Fâcheux*, which Molière caused to be played on the terrace.

On the 17th August, the King was at Vaux, his heart full of bitterness unceasingly stirred up by Colbert, and already resolved on the ruin of his host. On the 5th September, the Superintendent was arrested, imprisoned and sent to Pignerol, where he died nineteen years later. Louis XIV pursued his vengeance. He had hundreds of trees transported from the park to Versailles and the Tuileries, and the

above left: FOUCQUET, WHO
COMMISSIONED THE HOUSE;
above: LE NÔTRE, WHO
DESIGNED THE GARDEN;
left: LOUIS XIV WHO SEIZED
THE PROPERTY

paving of the salon taken to the Louvre; he seized the tapestries, the
brocade furnishings, the pieces of silver-gilt. Henceforth, Le Nôtre,
Le Brun, Girardon, Molière, would live within the royal orbit. It is
to their honour that they always retained their friendship and admiration for their benefactor. But the monarch never forgave.

Eventually, Vaux was returned to Madame Foucquet, the most
active and most intelligent defender of her husband, and she exhausted herself in vain efforts to secure his liberation. After the death of
her son, the château was bought by Maréchal de Villars, who decorated the façade with his coat of arms; where, however, the celebrated squirrels, emblems of the Superintendent, still remain under the
coping.

The third purchaser of Vaux was the Duc de Choiseul Praslin,
whose descendants retained it through the vicissitudes of the Revolu-
tions until 1873. The restoration undertaken by Duke Theobald through
the architect Visconti in 1842 was made with knowledge and good
taste; but the gardens remained neglected, the sheets of water dry
and the statues dilapidated. The estate was put up for sale and was
bought by M. Alfred Sommier. It is to him, to his son and to the latter's widow, Madame Edmée Sommier, that we owe the admirable
restoration of the original whole, made with great knowledge and
a scrupulous care for accuracy. The architects Lainé and A. Duchene
were their principal collaborators.

For those who enjoy gardens in the French style, Vaux is the
supreme example. The park abuts onto a hill, whose lower slope, supported by the grotto with seven arcades, becomes a terrace. A little
higher up, stands the great and gilded statue of the Farnese Hercules.
Leading to this point are canals, paths, decorative flowerbeds and
turf, whose lay-out is conceived so that it may be seen from the flight
of steps. Looking back from the foot of the steps, only the château
is visible, but from further away, the outbuildings and pavilions of
the Court of Honour gradually emerge as part of the principal building, unfolding themselves round it like a fan. A few steps more, and
one discovers what up to then has been unperceived: two transversal
canals, at the ends of which are revealed the trelliswork of water which
includes three terraces ornamented with basins and fountains; and
on the other side, the entrance to the kitchen-garden and to a grotto
known as 'the Confessional'. Further on is a third canal, of very large
dimensions, which, from its rounded end, is called 'the Frying Pan'.
Thus new perspectives astonish the stroller who in a first glance from
the steps, had thought the whole park visible.

The principal room of Vaux-le-Vicomte is the oval salon under
the dome. To right and to left, other salons, of pleasantly habitable
size, are ornamented with gilding, with painted ceilings, with books
and fine furniture. Not much of the original furniture remains, but
poor Foucquet could not have been less than charmed with the pieces
placed there by the last owners of the place, so perfect is their choice.
The splendour of Vaux-le-Vicomte is warm. The continual occupation
of the house as a private dwelling gives it a particular grace.

Jacqueline de Chimay

opposite: THE LIBRARY

A BRONZE STATUETTE OF HERCULES

The magnificence
of the interior
does not destroy its friendliness

THE BILLIARD-ROOM, DECORATED BY LE BRUN

right: THE STATE BEDROOM OF LOUIS XIV

CEILING OF THE STATE BEDROOM, 1660

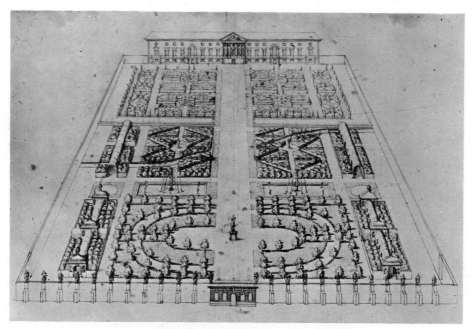

THE GARDEN ABOUT 1633 AND THE FAÇADE AS ORIGINALLY DESIGNED

Wilton

A classical scene created by centuries of discernment

TO MEN OF THE LATE EIGHTEENTH CENTURY Wilton was the house which, before all others, flattered the pride of English connoisseurship and artistic achievement. It had everything. There was a porch which was plausibly ascribed to Holbein; a grand façade and noble apartments which they knew to be by Inigo Jones; great paintings by Vandyck; a magnificent collection of antiques marbles; a Palladian bridge by the Architect Earl; and a triumphal arch by Sir William Chambers. In short, Wilton represented everything in English taste which was solid, tested and unassailable by tides of fashion. It was a classic.

The opinion remains just. It is true that we cannot allow the Tudor porch (re-built as a garden house) to be by Holbein or the south front to be wholly and absolutely by Jones; and we would have set more value on the original Tudor house than did those who allowed James Wyatt to rebuild it. But Wilton remains an exceptional composition of beauties – the pattern embodiment of the English patrician attitude to the classical arts through four centuries.

Sir William Herbert, first Earl of Pembroke, a tough soldier-politician under Henry VIII, was granted the abbey lands of Wilton in 1544. He built the house with the 'Holbein' porch. Here the second Earl held a court of intellect and genius in Elizabeth's reign. The third Earl entertained Charles I here and it was Charles who suggested the creation of a formal garden and the building of a

opposite: THE SINGLE-CUBE ROOM

JAMES WYATT'S GOTHICK CLOISTER, ABOUT 1800

FIREPLACE IN THE CORNER ROOM

new south front in the Italian style. In the course of the 1630s a spectacular garden was laid out and the Italian front began to rise. The garden is no longer there, but the classical front is. At least – part of it is there.

The front we see was, until lately, supposed to be a complete and personal work of Inigo Jones. On the strength of that supposition, as well as its intrinsic merits, it became one of the corner-stones of classical house design in the eighteenth century. Quite recently, however, Mr Howard Colvin, the Oxford historian, has discovered that its history is a good deal more complicated than we thought. It now appears that although Charles I, in or about 1632, advised the third Earl to employ Inigo Jones, that celebrity was far too busy with the King's own works to come to Wilton. He recommended a French architect then working in England – Isaac de Caux. It was de Caux, with Jones advising and approving, who built the south front of Wilton. But that is not all. As originally designed, this south front (it now appears) was to be more than twice as long as the front we see today; it was, in fact, to be only one of a pair of wings flanking an applied portico of six Corinthian columns.

It is odd to think of this famous façade as a mere fragment of a vaster composition. But how much in originality of character it gained by the reduction. When, for reasons unknown but most likely connected with the Civil War, the Earl decided to be content with less than one half of his architect's proposal, it meant that the admirable Venetian window with its shield and figures became the focal point of the design. The two pedimented towers appeared. Accident and genius between them created a new equilibrium.

In 1648 or 1649, this part of Wilton was gutted by fire. It was in the time of the fourth Earl who had sided with the Parliament in the war. With what may seem to us a sort of insolence he called in Inigo Jones to restore it. In 1632 Inigo had been to busy to come to Wilton; in 1649 he was too old. This time he sent his relative and pupil, John Webb, and it is to Webb, with the great man still commanding in the distance, that we owe the Double Cube Room. Designed to set off the family portraits by Vandyck and his school, it is a masterly architectural interior in its own right. Sixty feet long by thirty wide and thirty high, the Double Cube is a cream-coloured casket of carved wood up to the cornice; then comes a plaster cove, painted with cartouches, vases, garlands and figures by Edward Pierce, and finally a flat ceiling with moulded panels containing paintings by Emanuel de Critz representing the legend of Perseus. The immensely rich and elaborate fire-place is curiously un-English: it reminds one of Cheverny – and reminds one, too, that in Jones's last days at the Court of Charles I the taste of a French Queen, Henrietta Maria, had prevailed.

After this architectural exploit, with which as presiding genius Jones's name may still be associated, Wilton remained virtually untouched till the eightenth century. In 1705 fire visited it again and gave the eighth Earl the opportunity of rebuilding some of the older part of the house. He bought the Arundel marbles – first of the great

English collections – and formed the major part of the art collection as it exists today.

The last phase in the architectural history of Wilton began in 1800 when the eleventh Earl brought in James Wyatt. Wyatt respected Jones, but he respected nothing else about Wilton and set about a vigorous replanning of the whole fabric. He made a new main entrance on the north approached by a formal courtyard. He brought a triumphal arch which Sir William Chambers had designed as a park ornament and made an entrance feature of it. He tore out the 'Holbein' porch and rebuilt it in the garden. Finally he reconstructed the old inner courtyard and made it into a cloister. If Wyatt had done all this in the classical style which he could command more readily than any man of his time, his reputation at Wilton would stand higher than it does today. But he and his patron must needs be Gothic and we still cannot find Wyatt's Gothic either as clever or as evocative as his contemporaries must have found it (indeed, the years 1913-15 saw a determined attempt to release Wilton from some of his over-weening mediaevalism). Yet somebody had to make Wilton into a modern house, fit for the nineteenth-century Earls, and Wyatt's general plan is certainly admirable.

Visiting Wilton today it is through Chambers's ornamented arch, with Marcus Aurelius on top, that we enter. Then we meet Wyatt, traverse his cloister and proceed to the great interiors of which the Double Cube is the climax. The Jones façade behind which these interiors stand comes last. Before that façade and seen from the windows of these rooms is a stretch of lawn untroubled by paths or ornaments and extending to the river; and standing across the river we

THE VENETIAN WINDOW IN THE SOUTH FRONT

below: THE SOUTH FRONT, A CREATION OF INIGO JONES AND ISAAC DE CAUX

INTERIOR OF THE BRIDGE

see the other architectural show-piece of Wilton – the Palladian Bridge.

The expression 'Palladian Bridge' has for England a special meaning and all of it is conveyed by the bridge here at Wilton. There are two others, almost exactly like it, one at Prior Park and the other at Stowe; and none of the three is very like any bridge designed by Andrea Palladio. Andrea did, indeed, design (though he did not execute) a three-arch bridge for Venice with colonnades and a central portico, and our English type pays homage to this while turning it inside out and creating something wholly new within the general Palladian argument. The Wilton example is the first of the English group, having been finished in 1737. That was in the time of the ninth Earl, the 'Architect Earl', a nobleman whose interest in architecture was so intimate and practical that a number of important buildings have been attributed to him. He had a valued executant, however, in Roger Morris and nobody will ever know for certain whose was the mind in which the brilliantly original notion of the 'Palladian' bridge was born.

It is seen from the photographs that the bridge does not lie on the axis of the house but at the end of a path running beside it. Thus it is the object which attracts the visitor before he has become aware of the Jonesian façade. He approaches the bridge and, from its steps, turns to see the façade. He passes through and across the bridge, turns again and becomes aware of the bridge, the river, the lawn and the façade as one picture in deep recession. He may imagine the portico; he will scarcely regret the curtailment. He may picture the formal knots, tortured hedges and statues of the third Earl's garden; he will be happier with the lawn. Standing here he may reflect upon the way in which a scene so classical, so deliberate, so complete, has been accomplished not by the decisions of one mind at one time but by a combination of accident, selection, genius and the tides of taste.

John Summerson

THE BRIDGE SEEN FROM THE SOUTH FRONT

WILTON

VANDYCKS IN A PERFECT SETTING

'A CREAM-COLOURED CASKET OF CARVED WOOD'

A SETTEE ATTRIBUTED TO KENT

The Double-Cube
inspired by
Inigo Jones

right: THE FIREPLACE IN THIS MOST
FAMOUS OF ENGLISH INTERIORS

THE ROOM IS 'DOUBLE CUBED' BECAUSE ITS LENGTH IS EXACTLY TWICE ITS WIDTH AND HEIGHT

ENGRAVINGS OF THE WATER-APPROACHES IN 1694

Drottningholm

The white palace of the Swedish Royal Family

WHEN, IN 1662, the Dowager Queen Hedwig Eleonora of Sweden ordered her Court architect, Nicodemus Tessin the Elder, to build a country palace on the island of Lovö, she chose a site on which, eighty years earlier, King John III had built a small country house for his Polish wife. She intended that the chief approach to her new palace should be made by water. The walls of the rear elevation rise serenely from a terraced garden and are thrown back in reflection by the still water of the lake.

A steamer travels in less than an hour from Stockholm into a world of pale green foliage through which the Palace, almost startlingly white in the clear northern light, is first apprehended. Swans glide away with an air of dignified resentment, and there, dominating its surroundings, lies one of the most beautiful houses in Europe.

The Treaty of Westphalia, signed in 1648, placed Sweden among the great powers of Europe. It was time to break away from the grim traditions of the earlier Vasa Kings as they were enshrined, for instance, in the fortress-palace of Gripsholm, and to turn to the France of Louis XIV for inspiration. The long northern winter had ended. Tessin's design for the house was in the classical French tradition, and for the landscaping of the gardens he was inspired by Le Nôtre, who was making Versailles one of the wonders of the world. So the gardens of Drottningholm are orderly, symmetrical and civilised. Straight paths of red gravel lead past tidy geometrical flower-beds.

posite: THE DOUBLE STAIRCASE PAINTED BY D. K. EHRENSTRAHL

DROTTNINGHOLM

THE CHINESE HOUSE

below: GARDEN FAÇADE

between hedges arrayed with military precision, around statues of bronze and marble.

The Palace as we see it now, a central block terminating in two projecting wings, is the work of three generations of the Tessin family, Nicodemus the Elder and Younger, and the latter's son, Carl Gustav. The paintings on the ceilings above the sweeping double staircase and in the salon which bears his name are those of D. K. Ehrenstrahl, the greatest painter of seventeenth-century Sweden, and the Gobelin tapestries are of the same period. But Carl Gustav Tessin, on the orders of Queen Louisa Ulrika, sister of Frederick the Great of Prussia, added to the palace and embellished it in the Baroque style without in any way disturbing the harmony which is one of the charms of Drottningholm. The swains and shepherdesses of Chardin and Boucher smile down from the walls. The bedroom of Gustav III would be incomplete without the blue-and-gold Baroque alcove which is its principal feature.

While Louisa Ulrika was adding an upper storey to the palace which she loved, her husband, Adolphus Frederick, presented her, as a surprise, with a 'Chinese Pavilion'. This celestial doll's-house, known as 'Kina Slott' or 'China Castle', is one of the earliest examples of the technique of prefabrication which the Swedes have today carried to such a high point of perfection. It was brought in sections from Stockholm by water, and reassembled on the site with all the fashionable elegancies of *chinoiserie* combined with Swedish Rococo which

its decorator, Jean Eric Rehn, could devise. The octagonal room in the upper storey, so full of space and light, might serve as an example to most modern architects.

It is, however, a theatre which confers unique distinction on Drottningholm. Louisa Ulrika, a typical daughter of the age of enlightenment, decided that Swedish Court life might well be enlivened. At first embarrassed courtiers found themselves dragooned into acting plays and pageants, but in 1753 the Queen, tiring of amateurs, engaged a resident troupe of French actors, and a year later, the first theatre was built at Drottningholm. An Italian opera company under Francesco Uttini was imported to reinforce the French players: both companies delighted the Court and set out to train Swedish actors.

In 1762, as their Majesties watched an opera, a boy behind the scenes upset a cask of turpentine. The building caught fire immediately and the Royal Family narrowly escaped to safety. Undaunted, the King and Queen at once commissioned Carl Frederick Adelcrantz, the architect of 'Kina Slott', to build a new theatre. His beautifully proportioned building, undecorated except about the main entrance which faces the palace courtyard, looks like a Swedish manor-house of the period. It is the oldest theatre in regular use in Europe.

The interior, by the French Court painter, Adrien Masriliez, is as simple and effective as the theatre's exterior. Three hundred and sixty spectators can be accomodated on wooden benches which still bear the original place-cards by which the seating was regulated with

A PAINTING OF THE PALACE BY
AN UNKNOWN ARTIST IN ABOUT 1740

below: THE INTERIOR OF ONE OF THE OLDEST THEATRES IN EUROPE

DROTTNINGHOLM

THE GALLERY   THE HALL OF THE KING'S BODYGUARD, DECORATED IN 1694

THE ALCOVE IN GUSTAV III'S BEDROOM

proper regard to Court protocol. Thus, the King's personal Guard, the principal Lord-in-Waiting, the Master of the Horse and similar dignitaries occupied seats numbered from 1 to 17, while the last fifty-five seats were reserved for 'valets and barbers of the Court, members of the kitchen and household staff'. When Queen Elizabeth II of England witnessed Pergolesi's *Il Maestro di Musica* at Drottningholm in 1955, much the same etiquette prevailed.

The accession of Gustav III, in 1771, established Drottningholm as the centre of Swedish cultural life. The King, a benevolent despot whose assassination at a masked ball in 1792 inspired Verdi's opera *Un Ballo in Maschera*, was himself a gifted playwright and an excellent actor by any standard. Under his inspiration Gluck's *Orpheus and Eurydice* was presented at Drottningholm before a Parisian audience had been given an opportunity to hear it. During a great part of each year four performances a week were given at the theatre while, in the park beyond, Gustav organised tournaments and pageants, the brilliance of which are still legendary in Sweden.

With the murder of Gustav the lights went out in Drottningholm and remained extinguished for more than a hundred years. The last Vasa kings, and their Bernadotte successors, disliked the palace. The theatre became in turn a granary, an officers' mess, a vegetable store, a lumber-room. Then, in 1921, Professor Agne Beijer came to Drottningholm to look for a painting which might have been stacked among the rubbish in the old theatre. Beneath the dust and cobwebs he found the original stage sets from the days of Louisa Ulrika and Gustav III. The elaborate machinery installed in 1768 by the Italian Donato

opposite: THE BLUE AND GOLD STATE BEDRO[OM]

DROTTNINGHOLM

left: QUEEN HEDWIG ELEONORA BUILT THE PALACE;
right: QUEEN LOUISA ULRIKA ADDED THE THEATRE

Stopani, which enables the entire scenery on the large stage to be changed in ten seconds, was intact.

Thanks to Beijer, the Drottningholm theatre is again filled with talk and laughter, with music and poetry. By a strange coincidence, Jacques Mauclair's company from the Théâtre de l'Athéné in Paris opened their 1949 season at Drottningholm with Molière's *Le Mariage Forcé*. Two hundred and fifty years earlier, almost to the day, the Rosidor Company, the first French troupe to visit Sweden, had opened their season with the same play in 1699. The theatrical museum, housed in the theatre, which is based on the collection which Carl Gustav Tessin ruined himself in assembling, recalls the past of the European theatre as does no other museum in the world.

King Gustav V, whose famous grandmother, Desirée Clary, almost married Napoleon and became the first Queen Consort of the Bernadotte line, lived in Drottningholm during the last years of his long life and died there in 1950. Every summer it is a country residence of the Royal Family, the park one of the favourite resorts of the people of Stockholm. The palace is a living link with the past, but here the past predominates, as it should, over the present.

Ewan Butler

A CHINOISERIE CABINET

DETAIL OF THE CABINET

opposite: STUCCO CUPIDS ON THE HALL CEILIN

GRANITE PANOPLIES SURMOUNT THE ALBA COAT-OF-ARMS

Palacio Liria

The Alba town-house with its superb art-collection

THE NAME OF THIS MAGNIFICENT BUILDING shows how it came
into the hands of its present owners. For the title of Duke of Liria
(a small town near Valencia) was given as a Spanish honour by
Philip V of Spain to the Duke of Berwick, illegitimate son of King
James II of England by Arabella Churchill (sister of the first Duke
of Marlborough). This first Duke of Berwick and Liria was one
of Spain's best generals in the War of the Spanish Succession. His
great-grandson married into the family of the Dukes of Alba and,
on the death of the last Duchess of the old line in 1802 (celebrated
as Goya's patron and mistress), the already double dukes of the
family of Fitzjames gathered to themselves the proud and seemingly
endless titles of the Albas, of which the dukedoms of Alba de Tormes,
of Hijaron, of Montoro, of Arjona and of Olivares (Conde-Duque)
are only the foremost of thirty-two. The present holder of the title
is the only daughter of the last Duke of the Fitzjames family.

The Palacio Liria is in the middle of Madrid, a short way from
the Plaza de España along the Calle de la Princesa. It was begun
in the year 1770 by the architect Buenaventura Rodríguez. Sheltered
from the street by a large and woody garden, the house itself is a
severe but elegant oblong with two handsome façades. Each of these
consists of Doric columns in the middle and pilasters on either side.
Above, the arms of the family of Alba stand out on a granite pediment.

The entrance hall of the Palacio is a large light room, decorated
throughout with hunting pictures by the seventeenth-century Flemish
painter de Vos, and hung with various trophies of the chase. A

osite: THE SALA ITALIANA

COLUMNS AND PILASTERS DIVIDE THE GREAT FAÇADE

THE DUCHESS OF ALBA, BY GOYA

passage leads to the library, and thence to the ball-room, the Goya room, the dining-room, the print rooms and the duke's drawing-room, and the small room of showcases normally belonging to the Duchess. A magnificent ceremonial staircase of three flights leads upwards to the bedrooms, including the rich ducal bedroom.

The remarkable feature of this house is the superb collection of paintings unequalled in any private collection in the rest of Spain. Second only to the paintings are the Gobelin tapestries and the eighteenth-century carpets, nearly all manufactured in the royal tapestry workshops of Madrid.

The paintings in the Palacio Liria number nearly three hundred. Outstanding are the portraits. These include in the Goya room Goya's portrait of the Duchess of Alba in a white dress, the Countess of Montijo and her four sons, and Doña Maria Palafox Marquesa de Lazán. There is Titian's portrait of the great Duke of Alba, Murillo's portrait of his eldest son, Cosimo de Medici by Bronzino, a very fine Veronese (a portrait of Bianca Capello) and a portrait of an unknown man by Raphael. Isolated but not ignored in this glittering galaxy is one of several portraits of the Empress Eugenie (one of whose sisters married a nineteenth-century Duke of Alba) by Winterhalter. There is an interesting Annunciation by an unknown Spanish painter of the fifteenth century, with the first Duke of Alba, the donor, seen at prayer. Other paintings include a comprehensive collection of works by Fra Angelico, Jacopo Bassano, Caravaggio,

THE ENTRANCE FRONT

Guercino, Andrea del Sarto, Breughel the old and Breughel le Velouns, Poussin, Van Dyck, Rembrandt, Rubens and Ruysdael. This collection was chiefly made in the seventeenth century by the De Harot family, and would have been even more remarkable had it not been for the quarrel between Goya's Duchess of Alba and her sister and heir (the Duchess of Liria). The Duchess hated her sister and her sister's family so intensely that in her will – she died in 1802 – she made over to servants and friends nearly all the specially prized paintings and other treasures that were not entailed with the estate. Godoy, the Prince of Peace, intervened in the quarrel and succeeded in gathering together many of these paintings and selling them outside.

Of the leading owners of the palace, part museum and part residence, one might single out for special mention the last Duke of Alba, a distinguished historian in his own right, who found himself involved in politics, somewhat reluctantly, on several occasions. He became Foreign Secretary in King Alfonso XIII's pathetic last cabinet. He also became Nationalist agent, and later Ambassador in London, during the Spanish Civil War of 1936-39. During the Civil War the Palacio Liria was bombed in the course of the battles around Madrid, but all the paintings and the greater part of the other treasures were successfully preserved. After the end of the war, the Duke supervised the restoration of the Palacio Liria to precisely its original condition.

Hugh Thomas

A SPHINX AND CUPID FORM WHITE SILHOUETTES AGAINST THE GARDEN SHRUBBERY

159

THE EMPRESS EUGENIE BY WINTERHALTER

A Museum
within a private house

THE STAIRCASE IS MORE A WORK OF ARCHITECTURE THAN OF DECORATION

THE SALA DE GOYA

THE DINING-ROOM, HUNG WITH GOBELINS

opposite: THE SALA FLAMEN

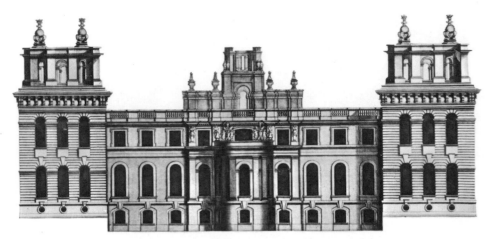

THE EAST FRONT: AN ENGRAVING OF 1717

Blenheim Palace

'England's biggest house for England's biggest man'

BLENHEIM PALACE, besides being a house, is a monument to British arms and a royal gift bestowed on John Churchill, Duke of Marlborough. From the first, its architecture was conceived as an elevated expression of the Duke's glory – or, perhaps, of military glory as an abstract quality; and the result is a performance more complex and intense than anything in English classical architecture, excluding only St Paul's Cathedral.

The house bears the name (anglicised from Blindheim) of the Bavarian village where on 13 August 1704 the Duke of Marlborough and Prince Eugene crushed the combined forces of Tallard, Marsin and the Elector of Bavaria. In February 1705, in response to the tremendous impression made in England by this feat of arms, Queen Anne announced that she would give the Duke the royal manor of Woodstock and replace the ancient palace there by a new building. The Duke was allowed to choose his architect and he chose Sir John Vanbrugh, a man of forty-one – soldier, wit, playwright and, by some favour of which we know little, the Comptroller (under Sir Christopher Wren) of the Queen's Works. Vanbrugh's experience of architecture was small. He had built himself a little house in Whitehall and was building the Earl of Carlisle a very big one in Yorkshire. He was accepted as a genius and such he undoubtedly was; the Duke could not have made a more fortunate choice. Nevertheless untutored genius alone would scarcely have been enough to build Blenheim, and we know now that the achievement is really due to two men – to Vanbrugh himself and to his collaborator Nicholas Hawksmoor, an architect of vast experience and with a vision in no wise inferior to Vanbrugh's. The two worked happily together and by 1707 parts of the great masonry shell were being roofed.

opposite: THE FOUNTAIN, IMITATED FROM BERNINI, AND BUILT IN

BLENHEIM

above left: JOHN CHURCHILL, FIRST DUKE OF MARL-BOROUGH; *above:* QUEEN ANNE; *left:* SIR JOHN VANBRUGH

The architecture of Blenheim lends itself to analysis as readily as a movement of classical music. Observe first the four identical towers – the heaviest elements in the whole. Bulky, rusticated, almost squat in themselves, they are additionally weighted by a load of piers and arches. Pinnacles fashioned as coronetted grenades flare at the corners. These towers are scarcely classical – they are almost as abstract as forts. The classical architecture of Blenheim moves in the space they define, depends on their fixedness for its mobility, on their dour inarticulacy for its power of rhetoric. Classical Blenheim is an affair of two of the five Roman orders – a fifty-foot Corinthian and a Tuscan less than half that height. Although Englishmen always think of Blenheim as very big indeed, fifty-foot is nothing much. Michelangelo's great order at St Peter's is more than double Blenheim's Corinthian, and Bernini's Tuscan in the piazza much more than double Vanbrugh's (which is worth remembering, for there is a curious echo of Michelangelo-Bernini in the total perspective of Blenheim in the main approach). But Blenheim seems big enough and is big enough to enact the drama it intends; and after all it is a *house* and its windows are the windows of rooms and not of a Cathedral nave.

It is, however, also a *temple*. The Corinthian order announces the

THE STATUE OF QUEEN ANNE IN THE LONG LIBRARY

THE SOUTH CORRIDOR

fact. Observe how in the centre block the whole fabric is articulated in columnar terms: there is no wall-space. All is pilaster, pier, column or impost. The portico moves forward in a movement of piers, not columns, and presents four piers and only two columns in its elevation; and the piers are in coupled pairs. This grave, massy procedure is maintained inflexibly on the horizontal plane, and then too on the vertical. The piers of the portico are projected upwards, as if through the pediment, reappearing on its raking cornice and carrying the sharp points of another pediment – the sharp points only, like the crags of an antique ruin; for this second pediment does not belong here but to the roof of the hall, rising behind and above the portico. This is a surprising, an outrageous, gesture and the miracle is that while it shocks it convinces. It is a visionary exaggeration but ordered by an unerring sense of grammatical expression.

The Corinthian order not only composes but penetrates the façade. It regulates the hall with four sentinel columns in its angles and emerges on the garden side of the house in another portico like the first but with an inscribed attic instead of a pediment and thereon the marble bust (captured at Tournai) of the conquered Sovereign, Louis XIV. The Tuscan order (not quite Tuscan but not quite Doric either) runs through the whole of Blenheim but does not always declare itself. It is resident in the entrance front of the centre block in the rudimentary guise of imposts to the lower windows. It emerges in the first projecture of the wings on either side, stops with a double beat before the curves begin, wheels through six bays to another double beat, turns, halts (a slower double beat) and enters the towers. Emerging, it marches through nine bays of colonnade and concludes in open distyles surmounted by trophies.

An English architect two generations later than Vanbrugh and of a very different school, Robert Adam, admired Vanbrugh for his 'movement' – exactly the word which this Tuscan manoeuvre evokes. Sir Joshua Reynolds admired him for the same quality, though he expressed it in different terms. Sir John Soane, again a generation later, found his 'bold flights of irregular fancy' enough to qualify him as 'the Shakespeare of architects'. Here at Blenheim this movement, this irregularity, this wildness of imagination is more evident than in any other of his works, perhaps for the simple reason that there is more room in which to exercise it. For one could continue the demonstration of Blenheim's 'movement' almost indefinitely – from the Tuscan to a massive rusticated Doric which controls the kitchen and stable courts; from the Corinthian to the strange abstract ordonnance of the towers. Or one could concentrate on the plan alone with its lively articulation – perhaps the first English plan which is expressive in its own right on the paper plane and (very naturally) almost the only English plan which has found its way into a French textbook.

Notwithstanding this, it is possible for Blenheim to disappoint. The great entrance front faces north and to visit it under a grey sky may be to stare unmoved at a sullen yellow mass. It needs the interpretation of light, and fullness of light comes only early and late

THE LOCK ON THE MAIN DOOR

THE GREAT HALL

THE ENTRY UNDER THE CLOCK TOWER

and sometimes not at all. Then again, to feel the intensity of Blenheim one must share Vanbrugh's and Hawksmoor's passion for the Roman orders and the emotional modulations of which they are capable; one must see the hall with its ranks of arches as something akin to a Roman aqueduct. For Blenheim is above all things an architect's house and it is useless to try to escape the fact, useless to pretend that the paintings by Thornhill and Laguerre in the hall and saloon are more than very able and appropriate specimens of their international kind; or that the other rooms at Blenheim – excepting only the splendid Long Library – contain anything one would remember for a lifetime.

As for the history of Blenheim from its building in 1705-10 to the present day, little need be said. It starts with the tragicomedy of Vanbrugh's quarrel with the Duchess, of how after years of vicious criticism and interference she left him with no alternative but to break with her and leave his masterpiece to be finished by others. The Duchess did live almost to finish it with Hawksmoor returning to build a triumphal arch to the Duke's memory and a magnificent column of Victory in the park. After that Blenheim in its two thousand acres of land was so fabulously magnificent and so utterly complete that it was difficult indeed for any of the Duke's successors to find improvements to which they could set their hands. There were, however, two – the fourth and the ninth – who made the attempt; but ironically some of the changes made by the fourth Duke were bitterly

regretted and the ninth Duke in part restored the *status quo*.

These changes were not in regard to the house but to the gardens and park. Vanbrugh's conception of the house had naturally enlarged itself into a formal layout of the kind which the early eighteenth century inherited from Versailles. Before the entrance front was a great court, before the garden front a parterre unequalled in England. A straight avenue struck across Vanbrugh's gargantuan bridge, a straight canal beneath it. All this remained until the fourth Duke, embracing with too much enthusiasm the naturalism of the later eighteenth century, dissolved it away. The Blenheim landscape today is the soft, vague, indifferent landscape of a park 'improved' by 'Capability' Brown. It has its qualities. It was a fine gesture to create an artificial lake beneath the bridge, giving it something worth crossing, instead of a monumental ditch. But the destruction of the parterre was a disaster and it was this that the ninth Duke sought to repair, with the aid of the French gardener, Duchêne, in 1925, by creating a new parterre on the west. There he erected an imitation of Bernini's fountain in the Piazza Navona, Rome.

Blenheim does not lend itself to change and to the fabric virtually no changes have been made. Nor has Blenheim in its 250 years of history found itself the background of notable events. Except indeed one – Sir Winston Churchill, grandson of the seventh Duke, was born there in 1874.

John Summerson

THE GARDEN FRONT

left: BLENHEIM IN 1745, THE GREAT COURT

BLENHEIM

right: THE SALOON, DECORATED BY LAGUERRE

far right: THE LONG LIBRARY

168

475 Heerengracht,

A fine example of a Dutch patrician town-house

NUMBER 475 Heerengracht stands by a canal in one of the most beautiful streets in Europe. Of Amsterdam's three main canals the Heerengracht's lies nearest to the centre of the city; it was begun in about 1660 for the expanding class of wealthy merchants, the ancient ramparts being destroyed for the purpose. Part of the magic of this street comes from the reflection of the houses in the water which makes it unmistakably Dutch in character. The houses are tall and narrow, and crowned with a lively and varied collection of gables – some 'clock', others 'neck', others 'stepped', and some simply pointed, each typical of a different decade of building fashion. On their façades they carry in sculptured relief porpoises, dolphins, or shells – symbols of the sea which the Dutch loved and upon which they then controlled the largest commercial empire known to the world. The engravings from Caspar Philips' *Grachtenboek*, published in 1768, illustrate the elegance of this architecture: in spite of modern building the Heerengracht has not lost the eighteenth-century character which Philips portrays.

In his engraving the imposing façade of 475 at once attracts notice. Built in grey sandstone, its effect is rich and dignified; but its character is not pure Dutch. The shape of the house, five windows in width, the parapet above, the double flight of steps, the 'stoep', which rises to a *piano nobile*, are what we expect to see in the heart of Amsterdam; but the details are not the Dutch details which would normally be found upon such a house. Its taste is distinctly French – sophisticated and light: indeed, in the twisted forms of its ornamental detail there is a foretaste of full-blown rocaille.

Removing in imagination the plate-glass windows, and replacng them by the smaller sash-panes of the seventeenth century, we see that the front door (which is original) is framed with good stone dressings and 'composite' pilasters. The classical faces carved in each of the capitals remind one of the later English decoration under the Adam brothers. The most beautiful feature of the façade is the pair of female caryatids, which flank the central window on the first floor with restrained voluptuousness. Their bodies are gracefully curved, their legs turned slightly away from the window, and their heads facing each other. Each figure exposes one breast, and their drapery is wrapped round the plain columns at the sides of the windows.

Unless the trees which line both sides of the canal are leafless, it is not easy to see the detail at the top of the house, but the cornice is a fine one. Concave balustrades sweep away from the reclining figures of a man and a woman to each corner of the house; in the centre, where we might expect to see a family coat of arms, the cartouche carries two cherubs playing with fruit – heraldry was rarely displayed upon a burgher's mansion. Above the cartouche is an armillary sphere in gold-painted iron – an emblem, familiar all over Holland, of worldwide commerce, and a reminder of the sources of the wealth with which this house was built.

It is to the family of de Neufville that we owe 475. As silk merchants and the leading bankers in Amsterdam, they enjoyed an important political influence; when their fortunes failed in 1763 with debts totalling three million guilders, the whole of Dutch commerce seemed affected until, with government help, sixty per cent of these debts were repaid the following year. In 1696 David de Neufville bought a house in the country, Heer en Berg, where Daniel Marot designed the garden. It was a few years later that the family bought 475 and Marot was almost certainly concerned in its building or redecoration.

Marot was born in Paris, the son of Jean Marot, a Huguenot engraver to Louis XIV; but at the age of twenty-four he had to leave France upon the revocation of the Edict of Nantes. He settled at the Hague and soon received commissions from the Prince of Orange, one of whose chief architects he became, working for him in Holland and in England. Marot, with something of the genius of the Renaissance 'universal man', was always influenced by France. Mathematician, painter, architect, engraver and designer, he was brought up in France at a time when her lead in the world of taste was unaffected by her

DAVID DE NEUFVILLE, BY MUSSCHER, 1696

THE DE NEUFVILLE FAMILY, 18th CENTURY,
BY J. M. QUINKHARDT

politics. Besides Marot's buildings, the extent to which he followed French taste can be seen in his published designs.

If Marot did not build 475, someone may have worked to one of his designs – perhaps his son, Jacob Marot. Two drawings for the stucco decoration of the staircase and hall are still preserved in the house. One is not signed but is known to be the work of Ignatius van Logeteren: the other is signed and dated – H. Jacob Hüsly, 1736.

The house contains the work of several generations – exquisite carving in the Louis XIV manner and a marble Louis XVI mantelpiece, which was carved for the house in 1782. One room contains *vedute di fantasia* by Isaac de Moucheron (1667-1744). But the glory of 475 is its Régence stucco work and staircase, from its Marot period. Immediately inside the front door is a small, square hall; two paces beyond lies the foot of the stairs, with its finely carved wooden bannisters. The hall is lavishly decorated in deep stucco, and yet it is not overloaded. One might feel cramped did not the mouldings create a sense of space and help to prepare the visitor for the climax of the staircase. It rises the full height of the house to a lantern, invisible from the outside, and like the entrance hall is covered with stucco mouldings in bold relief. Between 'gartered' columns and pilasters – a favourite Marot design which we again notice in the window-frames of the stables at the back of the house – the figures of Apollo with his lyre, Thalia with the mask of drama, and Euterpe with a trumpet, stand in fine proportion to their setting. Above there is a balcony in stucco which gives the illusion of a second storey, a kind of *trompe l'œil*, reminding one, even to the rug which hangs in folds over the balustrade, of a Veronese fresco. Sixteen figures are playing a diversity of musical instruments – flutes, mandolins, violins, violas, kettledrums. So dramatic is this vision that, for a moment, one wonders why the music cannot be heard.

475 was embellished by the Neufvilles at a time when they were casting off the thrifty habits of the seventeenth century. They were members of the Baptist sect of Mennonites and had led simple, religious lives until the beginning of the eighteenth century; then they began to use some of their accumulated wealth. We are fortunate that they had connections with Marot who so excitingly enlivened traditional Dutch forms with French ideas. 475 remained in private hands until 1907, when it was bought by the Hollandsche Sociëteit voor Levensverzekeringen as their head office. The magnificence of the façade and of the staircase has thus been preserved for us – an unforgettable contribution to the domestic architecture of Europe.

Colin Fenton

THE FRONT OF THE HOUSE IN WINTER-TIME

FAÇADE OF THE ORIGINAL STABLES
BEHIND THE HOUSE

THE FULL RANGE OF THE HEERENGRACHT IN 1770, BY CASPAR PHILIPS
475 IS THE HOUSE MARKED 'A'

173

A ROOM ON THE FIRST FLOOR

The mouldings
create a sense of space

DETAIL OF A FIREPLACE

THE CORRIDOR ON THE FIRST FLOOR

opposite: THE UPPER PART OF THE STAIRCASE W

THE ENTRANCE FRONT

Palais Schwarzenberg

The grandson preserves the deeds of his ancestors

OUR GENERATION knows only too well the enormous relief which peace and security can bring to a country that has suffered a long war. With their great victories in 1683 the Imperial army and its allies freed the city of Vienna from the Turkish menace, and the enemy's retreat to the East across Hungary finally lifted a burden that had weighed heavily upon the Austrian people. Their fear and uncertainty now gave way to a spirit of enterprise and a cultural resurgence that was particularly manifest in their architecture. Vienna was gradually transformed into the beautiful Imperial city that became renowned in song. Every effort was made to emphasise its importance as the Imperial residence and capital of the empire. Ministers, generals and officials of the court embellished their palaces to match the pomp and splendour of the immediate entourage of the Emperor. Vienna became one great building site. All the houses in the outskirts of the city that had been destroyed by fire or suffered from the invader had first to be rebuilt. From 1690 onwards Vienna was encircled by a great garland of lovely palaces.

One of the first patrons of this architectural revival was the famous Field-Marshal Prince Eugene of Savoy (1663-1736). When the Prince bought a site for his summer palace, the Belvedere, on a gently sloping hillside facing south from the town, the President of the Imperial Council of War, Count Heinrich von Mansfeld and Prince von Fondi, almost simultaneously acquired a vineyard in the immediate vicinity for his own future palace. He did not engage the Imperial architect Fischer von Erlach, but entrusted the work to Lukas von Hildebrandt (1668-1745), who was also to erect the Belvedere. He was less known in Vienna at the time, but soon became Fischer's great rival. For several decades, when the two men were at the height of their powers, Vienna was destined to inspire and fulfil the artistic aspirations of the baroque style that was to have a leading influence on contemporary architecture in Europe, particularly in Germany.

With Prince Fondi's commission, Hildebrandt started on his first garden-palace in Vienna. He was not destined to complete the work, nor was it the Prince's good fortune to see his ambitious wish fulfilled. The story circulated in Vienna that his design was to surpass even the Emperor Leopold I's favourite residence, the nearby Favorita, but when Prince Fondi died in 1715 there was still a great deal to be done. A year later, the Prince's daughters sold the palace to Adam Franz Prince Schwarzenberg (1680-1732). An early record shows that by then only the western half of the building had been fully furnished while the eastern half remained incomplete. The new owner terminated the contract made with Hildebrandt and appointed no less an artist than Fischer von Erlach to direct the work. So this famous building combines the ideas of the two great rivals.

For the decoration of the palace, Prince Schwarzenberg commissioned the great Austrian fresco painter, Daniel Gran, who first came to the Schwarzenberg family as a domestic servant. It is said that he was employed as a young kitchen hand, and when the Prince discovered his talent for painting he was sent to Venice for his education. By the time Gran returned the construction of the palace was sufficiently advanced to give him full scope for the knowledge he had acquired and to show his gratitude towards his benefactor. His first work in 1725 was on the dome of the great central hall where his creation, *The victory of light over darkness*, gave his princely patron so much satisfaction that it was followed a year later by another contract to decorate the gallery of the East wing of the palace. Though a bomb destroyed the great fresco of the domed hall in February 1945, the magnificent paintings on the wall in the gallery escaped damage by a miracle. The room is without doubt among the most colourful interiors of Austrian baroque. The theme of these brilliantly coloured frescoes with their many figures, so typical of baroque, is the triumph of Apollo, the god of the arts and sciences, the guardian of truth, goodness and beauty. Besides Gran's monumental frescoes and gorgeous stuccoes, the gallery is also remarkable as the only one in Vienna that has retained its original pictures. Among the finest works of art in the Palais Schwarzenberg are two precious paintings, *The kidnapping of Ganymede* by Rubens, a glorious picture dating from 1610-11, and the impressive male portrait of Antonello da Messina from 1475. The outstanding quality of the Persian carpets in this palace could hardly be matched in any other princely collection. All of them belong to the Golden Age of this art, the sixteenth and seventeenth centuries, but the most valuable piece is the famous Medallion carpet showing a garden scene with all kinds of plants and animals.

The garden was planned on architectural lines, like those of all baroque summer places. In 1783 it was transformed into an English park. The observant visitor today can still clearly see traces of the

'AUTUMN', ONE OF MATTIELLI'S FOUR FIGURES REPRESENTING THE SEASONS

A FOUNTAIN IN THE PARK

work of the landscape gardener J. P. Trehet, who was summoned
from Paris to plan the garden of Schönbrunn. But Hildebrandt, and
later Fischer and Gran, also altered the original design. The gentle
slope in front of the palace was transformed into great parterres,
ramps, terraces, fountains and ponds like their Italian and French
models. To the foreign plants which he acquired, Prince Schwarzenberg added the statues by the court sculptor Lorenzo Mattielli and
other ornaments that made his garden unique in Vienna. Fortunately
many of the figures are still in quite good repair, like the allegorical
representation of the four seasons and the famous Raptus group depicting mythological rapes. The Raptus figures, in particular, belong to
the most skilfully executed examples of Viennese garden sculpture,

THE FAÇADE FACING THE PARK

179

A STOVE IN THE WRITING-ROOM

THE CENTRAL HALL BELOW THE DOME

DETAIL OF GRAN'S GALLERY IN THE
EAST WING

for they combine liveliness and grace with a decorative quality that makes them a wonderful subject for photography.

Thanks to the enormous wealth derived from his vast possessions in Bohemia, and the dignity of his position as Court Marshall, Prince Schwarzenberg had all the means at his disposal to complete his palace in the style and manner that reflected the ideals and qualities of a *grand seigneur*. He died from injuries resulting from an error of judgement on the part of the Emperor Karl VI, while hunting with the Court.

The Schwarzenbergs belonged to one of the most noble families of the Holy Roman Empire and the Austrian monarchy. In the great square named after him in front on the palace is the equestrian statue of the Field Marshal and statesman, Prince Karl Philipp, who was Commander-in-Chief of the allied armies at the battle of Leipzig in 1813. His nephew, Prince Felix (1800-1852) was the first Prime Minister to the young Emperor Franz Josef, while his brother Friedrich (1809-1885) rose from Archbishop in Salzburg and Prague to become one of Austria's greatest Cardinals.

The beautiful palace suffered damage during the bombing of Vienna on 21 February 1945. Although the political upheavals of our generation have robbed his family of their extensive properties in Bohemia, the owner of the house today, Prince Henry Schwarzenberg, considered it his duty to carry on the great traditions of princely patronage, and by the end of 1957 completed his tremendous task of restoration. On the medal that was cast to mark this happy occasion can be read the words: *Avi servare gesta nepotem decet* – 'It befits the grandson to preserve the deeds of his ancestors'.

Franz Windisch-Graetz

opposite: THE FAMOUS PERSIAN CARPET, KNOWN AS THE MEDALL CARPET, ONE OF THE GREAT TREASURES OF SCHWARZENBE

THE FAÇADE IN THE EIGHTEENTH CENTURY

Palazzo Labia

A Venetian palace immortalized by Tiepolo

THE LABIA WERE RICH, foreign upstarts in a city ruled by the oldest noble families in Europe. They bought their way into the Venetian aristocracy in 1646 when this became possible for the first time owing to the State's desperate financial crisis brought about by the war with Turkey. Thereafter, until the fall of the Republic, they compensated for their lack of ancestors by a display of wealth that soon became their chief claim to renown and has remained legendary to this day.

At the beginning of the eighteenth century they built the palace which bears their name in the parish of S. Geremia overlooking the Rio di Cannaregio, the most important tributary of the Grand Canal. The architects they employed, Tremignon and Cominelli, are still little known. They showed their originality by breaking with the dramatic façades, heavy with detached columns, that had dominated most Venetian palaces since the late Renaissance and had reached a climax in Longhena's grandiose schemes for the Pesaro and other noble families. The façades of the Palazzo Labia are indeed equally rich in effects of light and shade, but much calmer and less powerful. There are three façades – an indication, in itself, of the fabulous wealth of the Labia, for most families were content to attach a noble front to that part of their palace which overlooked the Grand Canal and not bother too much about the rest. The Palazzo Labia, however, looks equally splendid behind from the large Campo S. Ge-

THE BALLROOM, WITH TIEPOLO'S PAINTING OF CLEOPATRA AND MARK
ANTONY AT THE HARBOUR

remia which it dominates, from the Cannaregio itself, and from the Grand Canal from which it stands back somewhat withdrawn.

The State rooms on the first floor surround the central courtyard, and these the Labia filled with a fine collection of paintings. Old masters, accumulated by noble families over the centuries, were clearly unavailable, but they acquired the best of their contemporaries, above all a large number of pictures by Luca Giordano, whose repeated visits to Venice helped to stimulate the great artistic revival of the eighteenth century. The ceilings had canvases inserted into them, and by 1750 the palace could easily vie in richness with any of its older and more aristocratic rivals.

Within it lived two brothers, their wives and mother. The elder brother, Angelo Maria, became an Abbé to escape political duties, but this did not prevent him marrying, though it may explain his choice of a commoner for wife. His main interests were literary. He organised a marionette theatre which caused something of a stir, for there were real singers concealed behind the scenes to perform the parts. He also wrote savage satires in Venetian dialect on such few signs of change and new ideas as could be seen in the stagnant society around him. In his later years he showed his devotion to conservative ideas in a more practical way by sending secret reports of any potentially subversive conversations he had overheard to the dreaded Inquisitors. But even he was forced to recognise that life was no longer what it had been, and in the most beautiful line of poetry written in Venice during the eighteenth century, he revealed the sadness that underlay the fabulous ceremonies that still attracted the tourists. After describing the glories of the Regatta of 1775 (*Che Canal, che tragheti! oh Dio, che Donne!*), he ends with a sob:

> *E pur, non so el perché, mi piansaria*
> (And yet, I know not why, I wanted to weep)

His younger brother, Paolo Antonio, married conventionally into the old aristocracy, but he too took no part in public life. The most lively character in the palace seems to have been their mother. In her younger days she had been a great beauty, and her portrait by Rosalba Carriera was said to have been that artist's most attractive work. In 1739, well past middle age, she still charmed the critical French traveller Charles de Brosses, as she flirted with him and showed him her jewels, the finest private collection in Europe.

These were the people who in about 1750 ensured their immortality by calling on the greatest European artist of the day, then at the very height of his powers, to decorate one of the rooms in their palace. Tiepolo revelled in splendour and ostentation, and his frescoes in the *Salone* of the Palazzo Labia are certainly the finest example of his work in Italy. On one wall he painted that defiant manifesto of aristocratic extravagance – the moment when Cleopatra dazzles her Roman conqueror Mark Antony with the splendour of the entertainment she offers him by dissolving one of her pearls in a cup of wine. Tiepolo had treated the subject often enough before, but his choice of it here, so suitable as a symbol of the Labia's own position in Venetian

THE FAÇADE ON THE GRAND CANAL

THE DÉCOR REFLECTED IN A SPANISH MIRROR

Opposite: THE GREEN DAMASK SALONE CONTAINS HUGE ALLEGORICAL SCENES
POMPEO BATONI

PALAZZO LABIA

society, was surely dictated by the fame of his patroness's collection of jewelry. Maria Labia, 'femme sur le retour, qui a été fort belle et fort galante', probably found no great difficulty in identifying herself with the beautiful Egyptian queen.

On the other wall Tiepolo painted her and Mark Antony together at a harbour. It is typical of the Venetian artist's lack of interest in psychology that no-one is quite certain whether they are meeting or parting. A certain tenseness in Cleopatra's pose seems to suggest that some sort of farewell is intended. Above, the winds blow, the sail is fully extended, flags flutter in the breeze, a greyhound strains at the leash. On the ceiling of this great room, as if to lift these scenes into the range of legend and timelessness, Tiepolo has painted mythological allegories which have not yet been adequately interpreted. But no description can do justice to the room, for one of its essential features is the relationship of the spectator himself to the scenes he is watching. With his collaborator, the architectural painter Mengozzi-Colonna, Tiepolo has devised a scheme of infinite spatial complexity. The banquet takes place above a series of painted steps on which stands a dwarf, half in Cleopatra's world, half in ours. The illusionism is complete, and yet its teasing quality suggests something much more than mere virtuosity for its own sake – a world of enchantment as real and yet as elusive as that which still existed in Venice in 1750.

In the nineteenth century the palace fell into decay, and because

THE CLASSICAL VENETIAN INNER COURTYARD

PAINTINGS OF VENETIAN VILLAS IN THE SALONE P

of Tiepolo's unpopularity there were few to express more than conventional regrets. The greatest danger, however, came much later when the artist's fame was at its height. In 1945 the explosion of a munitions boat shook the walls and caused fragments of the Banquet of Cleopatra to fall to the ground. Since then some brilliant restoration has largely concealed the damage, and the palace has found a new owner, Don Carlos de Beistigui, who has brought back to it some of the grandeur it enjoyed in its heyday. Many of the rooms have been provided with splendid furniture, often acquired from less fortunate Venetian palaces, and among the pieces from the Palazzo Mocenigo is a writing table which belonged to Byron who lived there. Some pictures of notable interest have been acquired, in particular three huge copies by Batoni and other Roman eighteenth-century artists of famous frescoes by Raphael, Annibale Carracci and Guido Reni. Above all there are some superb tapestries beginning with a set of scenes from the life of Scipio Africanus woven in Brussels at the beginning of the seventeenth century, and including a fine series of Chinese fantasies from the Beauvais workshops and the 'Tapisseries des Indes' made for Louis XV. But beautiful as all this undoubtedly is, to-day as in the eighteenth century, the Palazzo Labia still owes its reputation as one of the great houses of Europe to one single room of fabulous enchantment.

Francis Haskell

A LOUIS XIV TORCHÈRE,
DESIGNED FOR VAUX-LE-VICOMTE

THE PRESENT OWNER'S TRIBUTE TO VENETIAN ADMIRALS

LOUIS XV TAPESTRIES IN THE SALON DES INDES

187

PALAZZO LABIA

THE CEILING OF THE BALLROOM

below: THE MEETING, OR PERHAPS THE PARTING,
BETWEEN CLEOPATRA AND ANTONY

Tiepolo's world
of enchantment

A TIEPOLO SPANIEL

opposite: TIEPOLO'S CEILING IS ARCHITE
TURAL PAINTING OF GREAT SUBTLETY

NYMPHENBURG IN 1701: ENGRAVING BY M. WENING

The Nymphenburg

The airy palace of the Bavarian Electors

THE ARCHITECTURAL history of the Nymphenburg extends from the year 1664 until 1758 when the last building in the *Rondell* was finished. It was conceived as a summer residence in the country; but today it is part of the outskirts of Munich, and accessible to all by a twenty-minute ride in a tramcar.

Four successive generations of the Wittelsbachs are responsible for it in its present form. The five-storeyed central block, a lynch-pin holding together an immense arc of variously-sized edifices, always joined, but often only by a stretch of wall eaved with ancient red tiles, was built by Agostino Barelli for Adelaide of Savoy. It was a gift from her husband, the Elector Ferdinand Maria, on the occasion of the birth of their son Max Emmanuel. They had plenty of space and grandeur already in their Residenz in the centre of Munich; but what the princess – a devotee of rural delights long before Marie Antoinette – now wanted was a summer villa. It was to be called Nymphenburg in honour of the goddess Flora and her nymphs. An engraving by M. Wening in 1701 shows the central block very much as it is today, with its balustraded double staircase above the three arches, but without the six fine central windows, beneath three smaller oval ones, which now ornament the façade.

The Nymphenburg assemblage, as one might call it, has the modesty of a manor house, rather than the magnificence of a grand-ducal palace. When the grand duchess died, in 1676, E. Zucalli had already been asked to complete Barelli's work. Her son, Max Em-

opposite: DISTANT VIEW OF THE HOUSE FROM THE GREAT FOUNTA[

manuel, succeeded his father as Elector three years later, in 1679; and in 1701 he employed another Italian, A. Viscardi, to add two further blocks, either side of the central one, and joined to it by windowed corridors, running above an arcade through whose arches one can glimpse parkland and flower beds.

For ten years Max Emmanuel was occupied with the War of the Spanish Succession. But when it ended in 1714 he immediately instructed the Bavarian architect, J. Effner, who had studied in Paris, to draw up plans for the further glorification of the 'villa' which his mother had loved so well. It was decided that the central hall should be carried up through several storeys, and six highly arched windows introduced into the façade to light it. Further rectangular buildings were planned for either end of the existing structure; at the south end, stables and official quarters; at the north, an Orangerie and Clock Tower (only completed by Max Emmanuel's son, Karl Albrecht, who followed his father as Elector in 1726). In this way Effner brought into being the immense *cour d'honneur* which achieved its present vast proportions and became a *Rondell* when Karl Albrecht's successor, Max Josef III, added three further separated building on either side, linked together by connecting walls. In 1761, he moved

THE AMALIENBURG, BY F. CUVILLIÉS, 1734-1739

above and right: AMALIENBURG: ORNA-MENTATION OF THE SPIEGELSAAL

...osite: AMALIENBURG: VIEW FROM THE ...ROOM TO THE SPIEGELSAAL

THE NYMPHENBURG

NYMPHENBURG: MINIATURE BY M. VON GEER, 1730

PLAN OF THE FRENCH GARDEN, ABOUT 1720

the Royal porcelain factory, which he had founded some years before, into one of these modest and agreeable edifices.

Despite the fact that it took long to build, and was exposed to many architectural influences, Italianate, French, baroque, rococo, and that, in the early nineteenth century, its formal baroque garden was transformed into the style of an English park, the Nymphenburg possesses simplicity, charm and integrity. From whichever direction one approaches, the eye travels towards it along an avenue of water. On the side of the *Rondell* this ends presently in a huge final basin from which a fountain throws a white jet high into the air.

The buildings round the huge crescent are low upon the horizon and could never be called pretentious. Karl Albrecht envisaged a town ('Karlstadt') behind them, with the palace as its nucleus; but this project never came to anything. The rooms of the Nymphenburg are impressive; slightly less restrained than the exterior; but Effner's wealth of decoration, the stucco ornament and brightly-hued paintings by the seventy-year-old Zimmermann and his son Franz, in their varied framework of white and gold, avoid actual exuberance. We see Diana and other Olympian divinities paying delicate attention to Flora. Here is Kephalos and Procris, Mars and Venus, and delightful pastoral scenes over the doors. In the long north and south galleries can be found a whole series of huge oil paintings of the Nymphenburg and of other Wittelsbach palaces. The Great Hall, which was used for court ceremonies and for concerts under the music-loving Max III Josef, was partitioned in 1756 at the suggestion of Cuvilliés, and three lofty arches reveal a balustrated gallery of great lightness and charm.

Max Emmanuel discerned Cuvilliés' talent and enabled him to develop it. The future court architect had begun as court dwarf. He was then aged eleven. Max Emmanuel soon detected his talent, apprenticed him first to Effner in Munich and then sent him to Paris in 1720 to study for five years under the famous Blondel, who was still a very young man. The Elector was amply recompensed, perhaps most of all when Cuvilliés erected the little Residenz theatre in Munich for him. It has recently arisen, like some white and gold phoenix from the flames, remodelled by hands which seem to have kept all the rococo cunning, so that we have an interior more beautiful even than that of the little Opernhaus of the Margravine in Bayreuth.

This theatre for many of us is Cuvilliés' masterpiece, but the title is generally given to the Amalienburg, which has long been regarded as 'the immortal creation of Bavarian rococo'. Cuvilliés was peculiarly fitted to unite French lightness and grace with German sensitivity to plastic form. The Amalienburg is the third and most famous of the pavilions in the grounds of the Nymphenburg. The other two are the Pagodenburg (1716-19) and the Badenburg (1718-21), both built by Effner, and both well worth the walk through the wood; the former for the light it throws on the eighteenth-century love of *chinoiserie*, the latter for its cool and restful simplicity and for its very early version of an indoor swimming pool.

The Amalienburg, more ambitious than either of these, was built as a hunting lodge and picnic resort for another electress,

THE ENTRANCE FRONT

Maria Amalia, wife of Karl Albrecht, the chosen head of the Holy Roman Empire. The Amalienburg was begun in 1734 and finished in 1739. The focal point of this little treasure of architecture is its central Hall of the Mirrors, glittering with a white and icy splendour, and where a wonderful use of rocaille themes has been made in silver. On either side of this graceful circular room with its many glittering mirrors, which give it an air of cold, almost glacial, magnificence, are a group of smaller rooms, four on one side, three on the other. There is the *Hündekammer* with its seven or eight arched recesses for spaniels under the gun-cupboards. The corresponding room on the other side is the kitchen, panelled with blue and white Delft tiles which depict flowers and scenes of everyday life in China and with a ceiling ornamented with blue and white *chinoiseries*. The interior decoration of the Amalienburg was carried out, to Cuvilliés' designs, by J. B. Zimmermann and by Joachim Dietrich, a Munich master of woodcarving. But some of it may have been done by E. Zerhelst the Elder, a Dutch sculptor, who may have contributed the plastic nude figures above the main entrance and on the cornice of the Hall of Mirrors.

The Bavarian monarchy, founded under the aegis of Napoleon, vanished in turn after a little over a hundred years of existence. The Wittelsbachs still have the right to occupy the south wing, and occasionally it is exercised by Herzog Albrecht, son of Grand Prince Rupprecht. When he gives a personal reception there, the shades of his many ancestors who had so great a love of building, may gather in the darkness amongst the trees, gazing with approval upon the novelty of a floodlit fountain.

Monk Gibbon

above left: ELECTOR FERDINAND-MARIA; *above:* GRAND DUKE KARL ALBRECHT; *left:* GRAND DUCHESS MARIA AMALIA

195

THE CEILING OF THE GREAT HALL

The Nymphenburg is the lightest of Baroque palaces

THE KITCHEN IN THE AMALIENBURG

right: THE CHINESE ROOM IN THE NYMPHENBURG

opposite: NYMPHENBURG: A CORNER OF THE GREAT HA

THE CENTRE OF THE HOUSE IN THE LATE EIGHTEENTH CENTURY

Stupinigi

Juvara's hunting-lodge in Piedmont

THE PALAZZINA DI CACCIA (hunting lodge) of Stupinigi stands a
few miles outside Turin. It was begun in 1729 by the architect Filippo
Juvara, whose most ambitious work it undoubtedly was. He worked
under the instructions of the first King of Sardinia, Vittorio Amedeo II.
The King strove to live in the style of his fellow eighteenth-century
monarchs and the *Palazzina di Caccia* is one of the fruits of this self-
consciously monarchical frame of mind. The palace was built on land
outside Turin which Vittorio Amedeo's Elizabethan great-great-grand-
father had given to the knightly order of Saints Maurice and Lazarus.

Vittorio Amedeo died, however, very shortly after Juvara began
his labours. Most of the work on the palace was therefore carried
on in the reign of his son Charles Emmanuel. But Charles Emmanuel
was more concerned with the practical rather than the architectural side
of monarchy. Indeed he managed, during his reign, to increase the
family kingdom by all of that section of the Duchy of Milan which
lies to the west of the River Ticino. The practical consequence at Stupinigi was that the architect's original grandiose plans were somewhat
abbreviated. The construction, furthermore, took much longer than
was originally foreshadowed. It was not until the last thirty years of
the eighteenth century that the building began to assume its modern
shape. New architects such as Ignatio Bartola, Birago di Borgaro and
Ludevico Bo took over after Juvara's death. Charles Emmanuel himself died. It was his son Vittorio Amedeo III who first used the palace,
holding there specially sumptuous parties for the marriages of his sons
in 1773 and 1781.

opposite: ORIGINALLY A HUNTING-LODGE,
STUPINIGI IS DOMINATED BY A HUGE STATUE OF A STA

VITTORIO AMEDEO II OF SAVOY

THE BALLROOM, AS CONCEIVED BY JUVARA
AND AS IT APPEARED SOON AFTER COMPLETION

HUNTING-SCENE
AT STUPINIGI
BY CIGNAROLI

The first period of royal occupation of the palace of Stupinigi was brief. Strongly anti-revolutionary in feeling, Vittorio Amedeo III rallied to the side of his fellow kings in the Napoleonic Wars. The whole of Piedmont was accordingly over-run by French armies. Stupinigi passed to private hands, becoming in 1802 a part of the University of Turin. Napoleon used it as a country house in 1803, staying there twice while supervising the formal annexation of Piedmont to France. The palace was also used for a time as the Italian residence of Napoleon's sister, the enchanting Pauline Borghese.

After Waterloo, Stupinigi returned to the royal family of Savoy, who continued to use the palace as a hunting lodge throughout the nineteenth century. In 1926, finally, Stupinigi was returned to the Order of Saints Maurice and Lazarus, who had all the time retained their ownership of the land on which the palace was built. Certain bomb damage was caused during the second world war. The pious proprietors have, however, restored it to its past splendour.

Stupinigi Palace is approached by a long drive through a formal French garden, at the end of which the central green domed building of Juvara is plainly visible. Drawing nearer, the gardens give way to a long series of colonnaded outhouses which lead past two court-yards to the hexagonal courtyard of honour. On the other side of the palace, the magnificent deer park stretches as far as the eye can see.

Inside the palace the chief glory is the *Salone Centrale* or ballroom. This is a long oval with a high dome. Four vast pillars rise to an elegant gallery. On the roof of the dome, Diana is seen leaving for the chase – a painting by the brothers Valeriani, completed in the year 1731. The superbly elegant stucco and frescoes make the *Salone Centrale* one of the most successful of all baroque interiors. The other rooms of the Stupinigi Palace open in four directions from this central jewel. The apartments of the King consist of an antechamber, a bedroom, a small salon (*salottino*) and the chapel of Saint Humbert. These rooms are adorned by frescoes of hunting scenes. Specially interesting here is the ornate decoration of the antechamber of the chapel to Saint Humbert. In the New Apartments (of the late eighteenth century), used most recently as a residence by the late Queen Margarita, the most dazzling painting is the *Sacrifice of Iphigenia*, by Giovanni Battista Crosato, on the ceiling of the ante-chamber to the Queen's bedroom, which itself is notable for the same painter's

opposite: ANTE-CHAMBER TO THE NEW APARTMENT[S]

STUPINIGI

THE DOMED CEILING OF THE BALLROOM, ABOUT 1730

THE BALLROOM, OR SALONE CENTRALE

cool and inviting *Repose of Diana*, also on the ceiling. Leading off the new apartments are a series of small rooms decorated in a Chinese style. Beyond these is a delightful Hunting room (*Sala degli Scudieri*) whose walls are decorated by Vittorio Amedeo Cignaroli's famous hunting scenes. Also in the so-called New Apartments are the Eastern rooms (*Appartamento di Levante*). This suite is decorated throughout in the style of Louis XVI. It possesses a Chinese room of great beauty. In a gallery of portraits otherwise devoted to the House of Savoy, Napoleon's coach, used on the occasion of his journey to Milan when being crowned, has found its last resting place. Finally there is the severely elegant bedroom where Napoleon slept in 1803. The bed itself is a silent monument to the Emperor's silent hours.

Hugh Thomas

opposite: THE GALLERY AT THE FOOT OF THE DOME AND ABOVE TI BALLROOM

THE BEDROOM WHERE NAPOLEON SLEPT IN 1803

A DOOR INTO THE LIBRARY

Harmony of taste,
variety of associations

LOOKING FROM THE KING'S APARTMENTS TO THE BALLROOM

opposite: THE CHINESE ROOM

THE GARDEN FRONT IN 1724, BY SALOMON KLEINER

Pommersfelden

The ease and spaciousness of German Baroque

IN ITS RURAL surroundings Schloss Weissenstein – more commonly known as Schloss Pommersfelden from the two tiny hamlets which neighbour it – is a surprise, and something of an agreeable anachronism. One drives out from the most charming and least spoiled of Franconian towns, Bamberg, whose theatre Hoffmann once directed, and where he wrote his fantastic tales, and the scenery is just that which he enjoyed: rolling country, green woods, vast carefully cultivated fields undesecrated by habitation, since the various farms cluster together in seemly groups. A narrow farm-wagon passes, drawn by two tawny-coloured cows; women ply the scythe, or hoe crops in the light sandy soil; and presently the brown outline of the great Schloss is seen, vaguely defined, far ahead against its background of low downland and dark green wooded hills.

Pommersfelden is magnificent; yet it blends peacefully with its setting, never disturbing for an instant the bucolic serenity which surrounds it. Owned today by Countess Ernestina von Schönborn (née Princess Ruffa-Scaletta) and her son, Count Karl von Schönborn-Wiesentheid, collateral relatives of its originator, it has kept something which Brühl and Benrath have inevitably lost. It is no mere relic, it still has a personal life of its own.

Lothar Franz von Schönborn (1655-1729) was Elector and Archbishop of Mainz and Bishop of Bamberg. He was infatuated with building. He admitted as much himself, saying that it was 'a craze which costs a lot, but then every fool likes his own hat'. He had chosen an expensive headgear. Most of his private fortune went

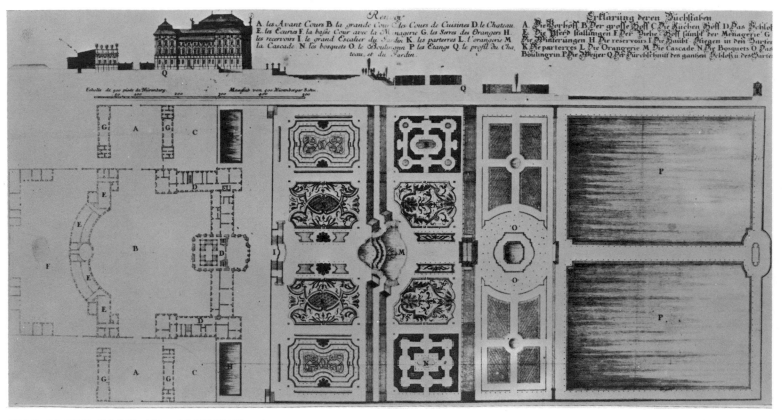

PLAN OF THE HOUSE AND GARDEN IN 1724

LOTHAR FRANZ VON SCHÖNBORN:
PORTRAIT BY HYANCINTH RIGAUD

either on it or on pictures. 'Building is a devilish thing', he exclaimed, 'once you start, you can't stop.' The portrait of Lothar, painted by Hyacinth Rigaud, with its double chin, tightened underlip and shrewd, crab-like, little eyes, is not particularly prepossessing, yet it manages to suggest the connoisseur and also the man of good will. What we hear of the archbishop is all to his credit. He is described as 'of an endearing nature, full of liveliness and humour, and every inch a prince'. The Secretary of War for the Netherlands, who visited him and who was noted for his critical nature, wrote that he was 'full of natural sweetness and charm and commanding everyone's love and respect'. He took a genuine technical interest in architecture and its theory. In collecting pictures he was not content merely to purchase old masters but also gave many commissions to living Italian painters. Every detail of garden architecture and administration interested him. He had had direct contact with the *Oberintendenten der Königlichen Gärten in Versailles* and was interested in the use of water and in the pruning and shaping of fruit trees. He wrote to one of his nephews, 'I get up at 5 in the morning, walk in the garden for a few hours and again in the afternoon and evening and with the greatest pleasure in the world'.

Lothar Franz's elaborate gardens, on each side of Pommersfelden are now a matter only for inference from the fine engravings made by Salomon Kleiner in 1724. But his stables remain, designed by Welsch in a great arc facing the main façade, with their line of stone figures and emblems sharply silhouetted against the sky, and with statues of Julius Caesar and Alexander on either side of the main door. In the centre of the arc and beneath the belfry is a circular hall which now houses four sleighs of early pattern and whose walls display frescoes by the Swiss artist Byss. Nearby, beyond a harness room smelling strongly of leather and with a formidable array of bits hung symmetrically upon a blanket against the wall, are no less than ten highly varied, yellow-wheeled vehicles of a past age, none of them as ancient as the sleighs or likely to have been occupied by Lothar Franz, but all of them reminiscent of that leisurely and privileged world which has passed away within living memory.

From the stable one can look across the sandy courtyard to the main building, which arose – a modified version of still vaster plans – between the years 1711 and 1718. The stonework of the Schloss, sandstone from the river Main, is mellow and sun-kissed. The central portion of the main block rises with impressive grandeur between its two projecting and protective wings. The architect was Johann Dientzenhofer, whose uncle had already built the Neue Residenz for Lothar Franz in Bamberg, 1695-1704. But both Johann Lukas von Hildebrandt, who was born in 1668 in Genoa and who died in Vienna in 1745, having contributed so much to the architectural glory of that city, and a Maximilian von Welsch, Lothar's protégé, also had a hand in it. The height and dignity of the main façade is stressed by the two pairs of lofty columns embodied in it. There is baroque daring in the two arched and gabled windows which flank the very fine pediment with its armorial bearings, surmounted by a statue of Mercury holding the aegis. Behind him rises a tiled and almost pagoda-like section of the roof. Similarly placed, but on the garden side, Atlas holds up the world (of intermingled circular iron bands) and this north-east façade, with its five high oval windows which help to light the lofty Marmorsaal, is almost the more impressive of the two.

The interior of Pommersfelden is one more refutation of the legend that all German grand-ducal magnificence is a shoddy imitation of the glories of Versailles. Franconian artistry and workmanship account for the greater part of it. Whispered accusations of plagiarism have been made against Zammels, the sculptor responsible for many of its statues, both out of doors, in the Sala Terena and in the north gallery of the staircase. But he anticipates Maillol by more than a century and a half. His Juno in a niche on the staircase is charming. His eight symbolic figures, the Four Elements and the Four Seasons,

THE GARDEN, OR NORTH, FRONT

THE CENTRAL BLOCK

THE STABLES, BUILT IN 1717

THE HEAD OF THE STAIRCASE   VESTIBULE LEADING TO THE MARMORSAAL

in the shell-decorated and slightly bizarre. Sala Terena or Muschel-saal, though they may be on the massive side, are rhythmic and pleas-ing and a refreshing contrast to the bijouterie of shells and crystals.

The staircase was by Hildebrandt. It has double approaches which unite in front of the Marmorsaal whose door is flanked on either side by niches containing statues. A second, arcaded, gallery runs above the first rectangular gallery, with its wide marble balustrade and supporting columns, almost like two separate *loges* in a theatre of the period. Far above one catches sight of Byss's ceiling fresco of the Four Continents, a forerunner of Tiepolo's famous work at Würzburg, which it may have suggested.

Pommersfelden with its four elements, four seasons, four em-pires, and four continents, may suggest bondage to the formal and even to the formula. But the reverse is the case. Two whole centuries have not robbed it of that ease and comfort and graciousness which its creator intended it to possess. The lofty Marmorsaal, with its deeply-sunk, upper oval windows, its rather cold, egg-shell wall-colour, and its grey marble floor, strikes a somewhat impersonal note. Where-as the Kurfürstenzimmer, with its bust of Lothar Franz in a niche and its ceiling painting of Ganymede by Melchior Steidl; or the long, open, sunny corridors where his magnificent collection of paint-ings are hung in what might almost be called prodigal adjacency – a private art gallery to show his friends, with Titian, Rubens, Breu-ghel and Dürer – as well as the rooms which house his superb library and collection of manuscripts; even the glittering and splendid *Spiegel-kabinett*, a blaze of gold decoration, of mirrors and chandeliers and with a particularly lovely parquet floor; are, all of them, plainly rooms meant to be lived in and loved; and the love which they have had in the past from successive generations still seems to be present and to warm them.

Monk Gibbon

right: THE MARMORSAAL, WITH ITS UPPER OVAL WINDOWS

CEILING OF THE MARMORSAAL BY ROTTMAYER VON ROSENBRUNN, 1717

NORTH-SOUTH SECTION THROUGH THE CENTRE OF THE HOUSE

THE GROTTO, OR SALA TERRENA, WITH FIGURES BY ZAMMELS

VIEW ALONG THE EASTERN WING FROM THE MARMORSAAL

left: THE STATE BEDROOM, ABOUT 1716

ENTRANCE DOORS TO THE SPIEGELKABINETT

The rooms of a man who loved what he created

opposite: THE FLOOR OF THE SPIEGELKABINETT

THE HOUSE IN 1794, FROM A PAINTING BY JANSCHA

Brühl

The pleasure-palace of an Archbishop

FOR WELL OVER a hundred and fifty years baroque decoration 'came to be a synonym for artistic extravagance and corrupt taste', but it has been restored to favour at last and in Germany today is producing a new generation of craftsmen who fully understand baroque and rococo intention and who can re-mould as well as re-gild *rocaille* ornament, as well as stress the brightness of rose-pink, sea-green and slate-blue 'marble' surfaces.

Two years after Clemens August, Karl Albrecht's brother, became archbishop-elector of Cologne in 1723, the foundation stone of the Schloss Augustusburg was laid on the site of the old castle at Brühl. The plans were by Johann Konrad Schlaun. He contemplated some thing relatively modest and in the style of the local, moated 'water-castles'. It was to be a summer palace and hunting-lodge, very different from the gorgeous building which later came into being, when the round towers of the western wing were torn down, the moat abolished and the Schloss became the *Château de Plaisir* which we see today. Even so there are traces of its thirteenth-century forerunner embodied in the walls and layout of the Schloss.

Brühl, like the Würzburg Residenz, was built over several years. There was this first period, which lasted from 1725 to 1728 under the guidance of Schlaun. Then Clemens August called in the aid of his brother's architect, François Cuvilliés. For ten years the latter acted in an advisory capacity and was responsible for nearly all the work that went on. It was he who decided that the south façade should open onto a great terrace and formal garden and that it

opposite: THE SOUTH, OR GARDEN, FRONT BY CUVILLI

should be the main front and linked up to an Orangerie. He designed the decoration, in white and gold, for the summer apartments, as well as the state rooms in the west wing and its façade. He kept Schlaun's general scheme but added much sculptural detail to it.

The third period in the evolution of the Schloss come with the arrival of an even more famous figure – the great Balthasar Neumann. Cuvilliés had kept Schlaun's staircase but the prince-bishop had decided long ago that, despite Schlaun's schooling in Italy, he was not up to contemporary standards. Neumann first came to Brühl in 1740. Cuvilliés had gone back to Munich in 1733. Much that he suggested was carried out after he left. It was under Leveilly, a local architect, that the lovely rooms on the ground floor of the southern wing were completed.

Neumann drew up plans for an entirely new staircase and a great dining-hall. He supervised the execution of them from Würzburg, first under Leveilly and then under J. H. Roth. Schlaun's staircase was removed and the new Stiegenhaus was created between 1743 and 1748. Most of its more gorgeous additions however had still to come. Roth was in charge at Brühl from 1754 till 1770. Von Stuber executed ceiling-paintings for the staircase and for the rooms to which they led; the Guard Room – really a reception room for visitors awaiting audience – and the dining-room with its charming railed gallery. Much of the earlier decorative work had been done by local artisans and artists to Cuvilliés' designs. But when the decoration of the great staircase began, Roth had under him for the stucco work Joseph Artario and Biazelli; who were followed later by Brilli. The latter carried out the great cartouche above the gold bust of the Elector, and also the pairs of giant caryatids, symbolising Music, Painting, Agriculture etc. who appear to be holding up the ceiling with their upraised arms. The most striking feature of the staircase is probably its four separate groups of figures supporting the vaulting either side; but its hand-rail of lovely ironwork, and the fascinating complexity of detailed decoration on the wall just above its flight, give it a lightness and grace – in contrast to the firm stability of these figures – quite as effective in its way as the simpler nobility of Würzburg.

In the great portrait of Clemens August by G. Desmarées in 1746 we see very much the secular prince, rather than the cleric. This was the aspect of his dual function of archbishop-elector which he clearly preferred to stress. For years he postponed going to Rome to be consecrated as archbishop by the Pope, since, so long as he remained unconsecrated, there was more excuse for the ambiguity of some of his behaviour. He was extravagant. He had at his Elector's Court a hundred and fifty chamberlains, a court fool, a court dwarf, and several Italian singers, two of whom were so lovely that the Pope is said to have summoned him to Rome to give an explanation of their exact status. We hear no backstairs gossip about the various members of the Schönborn family who achieved episcopal rank; but we hear of a natural daughter of Clemens August whom he married to her cousin who was the son of Karl VII.

We can see at Brühl many of Clemens August's possessions and

CLEMENS AUGUST, ARCHBISHOP OF COLOGNE

ENTRANCE FRONT, WITH
THE 13th CENTURY MOAT

CARLO CARLONE DID THE STUCCO
FOR THE DINING-ROOM

posite: THE GREAT STAIRCASE OF BALTHASAR NEUMANN WAS BUILT 1743-8

THE CEILING, BY CARLO CARLONE

The staircase at Brühl combines lightness with magnificence

TWO OF THE FOUR GROUPS OF STATUARY SUPPORTING THE STAIRCASE

the rooms connected with him. He had a blue-tiled Delft bathroom – later he made it into a writing-room – with stucco ornamentation in relief of various bath articles, comb, cauldron of heated water and so on. He loved falconry and a whole series of oil paintings of his favourite hawks are to be found in one of the long, cool, lower corridors at Brühl.

Those who visit the Schloss and don the immense felt slippers to cross its polished floors cannot leave without an inkling of what life in the mid-eighteenth century was like. The creator of the Schloss died two hundred years ago in 1761 on his way to Munich to attend the accouchement of a relative, the Electress of Saxony.

For four years, from 1809 until 1813, Brühl was in the possession of the French marshal, Davout. After peace was made it passed into the possession of Prussia and in 1842 it was restored by King William IV of Prussia. Today this architectural phoenix renews its youth once more, one of the finest survivals of a great period.

Monk Gibbon

right: STUCCO, SCULPTURE, IRONWORK AND MARBLE IN SPLENDID COMBINATION

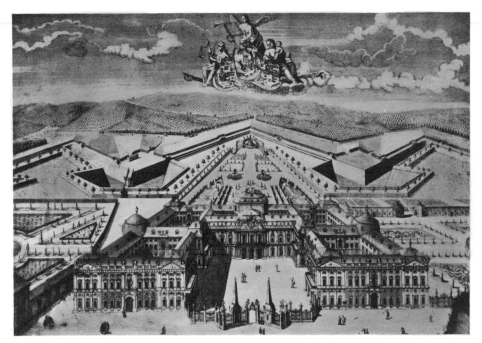

THE RESIDENZ IN ABOUT 1770

The Residenz, Würzburg

The highest flight of Baroque daring

PEVSNER HAS SAID, 'Between 1650 and 1750 Germany experienced a revival in art that brought her to the forefront of European music, to the forefront, too, of European architecture...'. With neighbours from whom she could learn and borrow, with native builders who had adaptability and a sensitivity to plastic form inherited from many generations of superb woodcarvers, she was peculiarly well-fitted to risk the higher flights of baroque daring. Lastly she had the inestimable advantage of enlightened patronage.

All this is demonstrated in the Würzburg Residenz. Many people were concerned with it. The French court-architects, Boffrand and de Cotte, were invited to advise at a preliminary stage. One encounters there the most famous of German architects, Balthasar Neumann, protégé of the prince-bishop of Würzburg, who began his career as a bell-founder, then became a military engineer and rose to the rank of colonel. He finally achieved a European reputation, having designed numerous churches and residences and even a new Imperial palace in Vienna. One meets Lucas von Hildebrandt, court architect in Vienna, and Maximilian von Welsch, who held the same position to the Elector of Mainz. One meets the Swiss-Italian sculptor and *stuccatore* Ludovico Bossi from Stuttgart, and his famous brother Antonio Bossi of Lugano. One meets, with his sons, Giandomenico and Lorenzo, the greatest decorative painter of his age, Giovanni Battista Tiepolo (1696-1770), whose work almost perished in the terrible

THE WEST ENTRANCE FRONT

air raid on Würzburg on the night of the 16 March 1945, when in twenty minutes five thousand buildings were either damaged or destroyed.

The foundation was laid in 1720, but it was not until 1750 that Tiepolo came to Würzburg to begin his three years of work, which were to put the final touch of genius to its interior. Of the four prince-bishops who occupied the see during the creation of the Residenz, two were members of the Schönborn family and nephews of Lothar Franz. Lothar himself was fascinated by the project and made constant suggestions, some his own, some emanating from his architects Dientzenhofer and von Welsch. His nephew, Count Johann Philipp Franz von Schönborn (1673-1724), had been made Bishop of Würzburg in the autumn of 1719. He had been an ambassador at various courts, and the Würzburg chapter – whose Domprobst he was – even before they elected him, were uneasily aware of his taste for magnificence. Since 1253 occupants of the see had lived across the river, in the Marienburg. But a fortress was not in keeping with the spirit of the time, and plans for a new Residenz in the Rennweg were begun immediately. The new archbishop seemed to know that his time was short and he would get up in the middle of the night, fetch a compass and study the plans. Lothar Franz remarked that Neumann would go blind, he was doing so much drawing on the plans.

Johann Philipp lived to see only one fifth of the house completed. Neumann had planned a frontage of five hundred and fifty feet, a court of honour, and two inner and enclosed courts. To these Welsch added later the two further side courts which make up the present fivefold assemblage. Johann Philipp's successor, Fürstbischof Hutten, was a scholar who did not contribute to the ambitious and expensive project. When he died in 1729, Johann Philipp's brother, Friedrich Karl (1674-1746), who had been Imperial Vice-Chancellor, was elected Bishop of Bamberg and Würzburg. On the 31 December, 1744, Friedrich Karl, who by that time was seventy years of age, witnessed the completion of the Residenz, although many of its crowning glories had still to be added by his successor Karl Philipp von Greiffenclau, who, after one intermediate election, became Fürstbischof of Würzburg in 1749.

Greiffenclau was responsible for some of the breathtaking features of the Residenz: the Tiepolo staircase ceiling – it is his medallion-portrait which floats amidst the clouds above the continent of Europe – the statues and stucco work by Antonio Rossi in the *Kaisersaal* with its vaulted ceiling and further masterpieces by Tiepolo; and the decorative work in many of the other rooms. But Greiffenclau deeply respected Friedrich Karl, whose coat-of-arms and portrait he placed above one of the fireplaces in the *Kaisersaal*, with his own above the other.

The uneven cobbled forecourt of the Residenz is no longer partitioned by the iron lattice work from the hand of the younger Oegg which was unfortunately removed early in the nineteenth century, but is still flanked at its extremities by two great pillars surmounted by a bronze globe and with the modern fountain which commemorates three of Würzburg's most famous sons, Walter von der Vogelweide, Tilman Riemenschneider and Matthias Grünewald.

The Spiegelkabinet and the rooms in the north wing, including that in which Napoleon slept, were wrecked in the raid, but the essential glories of the Residenz remain. They were saved by solid vaulting above the *Kaisersaal* and staircase – perhaps the most beau-

ONE OF TIEPOLO'S SKETCHES FOR THE WÜRZBURG FRESCOES

'PERHAPS THE MOST BEAUTIFUL STAIRCASE IN THE WORLD'

opposite: THE PART OF TIEPOLO'S CEILING WHICH REPRESENTS EUROPE: BALTHASAR NEUMANN LIES IN THE CENTRE, BESIDE THE D

WÜRZBURG

THE ENTRANCE HALL
TO THE RESIDENZ,
WÜRZBURG

tiful staircase in the world. Over the triple width of the dividing staircase and its wide surround on the floor above, is the immense expanse of Tiepolo's wonderful ceiling with its deceptive depth, which appears to rise in a dome, but is only about sixteen feet high. So huge is its area that Hildebrandt, who came here in 1738, distrusted this vault and said that he would hang himself from it to test its solidity. Neumann's reply was to offer to fire an artillery salute in its honour and to see if it would bring it down. Two hundred years later it was put to a very similar test and emerged triumphant.

Seen in the evening light the ceiling earns every panegyric lavished upon it. Almost apocalyptic in its eloquence, the individual figures and groups of figures of the four Continents are vivid and realist. In each a dominant female figure symbolises the Continent; but she is only part of the panorama which is packed with detail of intense interest. In the empyrean between these four impelling assemblages are the planets, symbolised by appropriate gods. But it is the human conspectus which has given the ceiling its unique grandeur.

The elaborate and complex grandeur of the *Kaisersaal* is a blaze of gold and colour. In the spaces between the deply-recessed and windowed vaulting, which Welsch planned to give the room additional light, Tiepolo painted the Emperor Barbarossa, Beatrice of Burgundy and a much earlier Fürstbischof of Würzburg. On the ceiling the god Apollo with his sun-chariot is drawn swiftly across the heaven by those deep-bellied charges which the artist loved to depict.

Neumann designed the walls of stucco marble and the three-quarter columns with richly gilt capitals. Antonio Bossi contributed the prodigal wealth of rococo decoration and the four charming stattues, Poseidon and Juno, Flora and Apollo, in paired niches at either end of the room. He began in 1749 with the *Gartensaal*, where Zick's ceiling painting, with its deep colours, integrity and Teutonic charm, precedes Tiepolo, but lacks the final exuberance of genius. Bossi decorated the *Kaisersaal* in 1750, the *Weisser Saal* in 1753; and, later, when, according to some people he was mad, he did the two symbolic groups of an old man, a young man, and a winged angel, which are now in the *Gartensaal*.

The Residenz is full of beautiful things, including tapestry from the factory founded by Johann Philipp von Schönborn in 1721 and taken over by Pirot of Frankfurt seven years later. The Commedia dell'Arte series have tremendous colour, humour and vitality. The Hofkapelle, a joint creation of Neumann and Hildebrandt, is strongly illustrative of the full exuberance of ecclesiastical rococo. There is nothing to suggest its existence from the garden outside. Neumann did not wish to disturb the symmetry of his southern façade. With its ingenious arrangement of slanting windows, its twisted columns, its two main altars one above the other, and its lovely gold-canopied pulpit and the other embellishments which the age permitted, the chapel is one more reminder of a time when material beauty was regarded as an appropriate illustration of its celestial counterpart.

Monk Gibbon

TIEPOLO'S PORTRAIT OF KARL PHILIPP VON GREIFFENCLAU

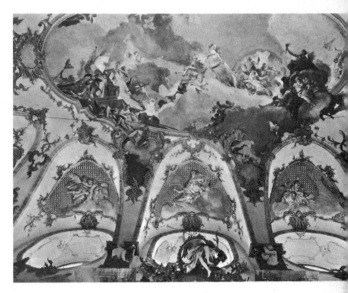
THE KAISERSAAL, WITH TIEPOLO'S PAINTING OF APOLLO IN HIS CHARIOT

THE GARTENSAAL. STUCCO BY BOSSI, PAINTINGS BY ZICK

THE WEST FAÇADE

Claydon

A smaller English country-house of delightful elegance

THIS IS BORDER COUNTRY, the border between the wet and stormy west of England and the flat wheat lands of the east. Approaching Claydon from Bicester, passing from Oxfordshire into Buckinghamshire, one leaves the ochreous Cotswold stone at the county boundary and comes into brick country. This too was the border between the Royalist west and the Roundhead east, the line running southwards through the Chilterns where consciences were searched most sleeplessly and where the best of the landed gentry took sides most anxiously and gave their lives most nobly. The Verneys, who had held land at Claydon since the fifteenth century, were desperately divided, one son supporting Parliament and accepting exile, the other killed fighting for the King at Drogheda.

'In 1611', writes James Lees-Milne, 'Sir Edmund Verney joined the Household of Henry Prince of Wales, on whose early death he was transferred to the service of the younger brother, the future Charles I. He is one of the truly tragic seventeenth-century cavaliers. A stalwart Protestant, he was convinced of the justice of Parliament's cause when the Civil War broke out. Yet he remained unshakably loyal to the King. "I have eaten his bread", he wrote, "served him for near thirty years, and I will not do so base a thing as to forsake him, but choose rather to lose my life (which I am sure I shall do) to preserve and defend those things which are against my conscience to preserve and defend." And indeed after the battle of Edgehill this gallant gentleman was found hacked to pieces on the field, his severed hand still firmly grasping the royal standard.'

Out of the plain rise isolated hills: on one of them, facing south beside the village church, Sir Edmund Verney had built a decent red-

CLAYDON

left: SIR EDMUND VERNEY BY VANDYCK;
right: FLORENCE NIGHTINGALE
BY SIR WILLIAM RICHMOND c. 1860

DETAIL OF NICHE IN THE NORTH HALL

brick mansion; and as the family, safely Whig, prospered under the Hanoverians, his great-grandson Ralph, now second Earl Verney, found himself in the seventeen-fifties with a draughty old house, and taste and money enough to rise to the occasion. He found a kindred spirit, in the farouche, eccentric, spendthrift amateur of architecture, Sir Thomas Robinson of Rokeby, sometime Governor of Barbados, whose design for a great stone west-facing façade, turning its back on the old brick house, itself showed most of these characteristics. Its eccentricity is obvious in the unresolved dualism of the design, with an enormous ballroom pretending to be one of a pair of two-storey houses and a central rotunda quite failing to dominate them both.

Some of the correspondence between architect and client has survived in an attic at Claydon, and shows more than the usual run of crises, conflicts, reconciliations, triumphs and disasters. Source of most of the disputes that enlivened the building, and of its final beauty, was a mysterious figure named Lightfoot, a freelance carver-decorator of genius, who played fast and loose with normal job procedure and made it necessary for Robinson to abandon the balls and breakfasts at Ranelagh (of which he was director and master of ceremonies) and drive down to Buckinghamshire to hold Lord Verney's hand more often than he had bargained for. A strain of fantasy in the Verney family, which produced in that century a pirate and a highwayman as well as the extravagant second earl, the element of megalomania in 'long Sir Thomas', and the 'no small trace of madness' which the latter found in Lightfoot, combined to produce the inevitable result: cracking walls, severed relations, financial collapse. Robinson died blind in 1777, but the work went on under Lightfoot until 1784, when Verney himself went bankrupt. The great rotunda and the shaky ballroom were taken down fifteen years later. But in his claim that he had left at Claydon 'two of the most princely rooms in Europe', Robinson for once did not exaggerate.

The house came through two women to Sir Harry Calvert, who took the name and arms of Verney and took as second wife Parthenope, the shy and scholarly sister of Florence Nightingale, who herself spent long periods at Claydon, writing her formidable letters, while Parthenope embarked on the first of the famous four-volume *Verney Papers*. The old house, with its Janus faces, matured and was Victorianised. Ivy covered Robinson's classic stonework and a pair of heavy-handed 1860 bays were inserted into the mellow Jacobean south front. The unfinished Georgian withdrawingroom was fitted out as a library; the gardens were walled, and cottages and bothies erected. Through the foresight of the Verney family, Claydon is now safe in the guardianship of the National Trust.

Driving up from the south or east, one comes between garden walls and cottages into the wide mid-eighteenth century stable court, somehow French in feeling with its rough grass and apple trees. Even from the lake on the west, Robinson's rather artlessly detailed façade belies its size. From the north one enters without ceremony, through the side door of what remains of the great classical house – to be

opposite: THE QUARTER-TON MARQUETRY DOORS OF THE SALO

astonished at once by the height of the ceiling and the delicacy of the rococo decoration.

Among the wonders of the Claydon interiors, the greatest are the North Hall, the saloon and the staircase. The North Hall is a double cube fifty feet long (ten feet less than the great room at Wilton) and in relation to the size of the house the sense of space is striking. Lord Houghton exclaimed of it: 'I like a room where one feels one can stand upright'. The walls and ceiling are lemon yellow, and the bold white medallions of the Doric frieze are set off by apple green. But the overwhelming triumph of this room is Lightfoot's rococo decoration, and the astonishing thing about it is that on walls and ceiling alike it is all carved in wood. Unlike French or German decoration of the period, it stands out against the plain wall surfaces with an effect of supreme elegance and grace, the conventional Chinese Chippendale involutions complemented by naturalistic birds and trophies of a quality unexcelled in Europe. One passes into the silver-grey saloon through magnificent marquetry doors, each quarter-ton leaf smoothly carried on only two brass hinges. The white wood doorcases are correctly Corinthian, and the atmosphere is more sumptuous but less romantic. Portraits of seventeenth-century Verneys in eighteenth-century frames cover the grey flock-papered walls, and above them runs a delicate Adamesque frieze. The library ceiling is equally fine, and is probably also by Joseph Rose, whose plasterers were later to flee in panic from the cracking ballroom.

One doubts if there was a single mind behind the splendid amalgam of frail marquetry and delicate ironwork of the staircase, poised beneath an oval coffered dome. The curtail step on the stone hall floor certainly has 'no small trace of madness in its composition', and suggests Lightfoot. The treads and risers are of mahogany inlaid with satinwood, teak, ivory and ebony; the soffits are elegantly panelled and inlaid, and so frail is the finish that few people now climb the stair to hear the famous rustle of the iron ears of corn against the wreaths and rosettes of the balustrade. At the top the sky floods down through a circlet of chinoiserie waves and sea-horses.

Claydon is as original upstairs as down. Florence Nightingale's bedroom, pale and wooden, is unexpectedly pretty, though not particularly feminine, and contains her only portrait, painted here. Next to it is a Gothic bedroom, pale blue and white, with Strawberry Hill doors and chimney-piece and three pink pentagonal Gothic domes. All the bedrooms contain fanciful examples of Lightfoot's carved rococo embellishments. Finally one comes into the Chinese Room, the first in England to attempt indoors the style of garden ornament brought back from the East by Sir William Chambers. The doors and door-heads, with their realistic caryatids, the twin chimney-pieces, the Canton bamboo furniture, are dominated by a riotous fantasy, a carved Chinese 'bedhead-grotto-pagoda'.

The house is full of music and children, the estate more intensively farmed than ever before, and Ralph Verney's magnificent orchards fill fifty acres of its walled gardens and nearer fields.

Lionel Brett

THE FRAIL MARQUETRY OF THE STAIRCASE

ALCOVE IN THE CHINESE ROOM

A DOORCASE   DETAIL OF THE FIREPLACE

The most fantastic example
of English Chinoiserie

opposite: CHINESE TEA-PARTY WITHIN THE ALCOVE

THE ENTRANCE IN 1826. ENGRAVING BY J. P. NEALE

Russborough

The Palladian façade of an Irish country-house

RUSSBOROUGH, built midway through the eighteenth century for the delight of one connoisseur, Joseph Leeson, 1st Earl of Milltown, has in the course of the last decade had the good luck to fall into the hands of another, Sir Alfred Beit. Whoever sees it to-day must be impressed by its triple graciousness; of situation, of architecture, and of unique content. At the same time it has an air of prevailing simplicity, which makes it not only a great house but very lovable.

It might be an Irish and more modest Nymphenburg, and actually it was built by an architect who came from Germany. According to Maurice Craig, Sir Gustavus Hume, a County Fermanagh gentleman, brought Richard Cassels – later to become Richard Castle – to Ireland about 1727 to build him a house on the shores of Lough Erne. He had been born in Hesse-Cassel, possibly of French extraction deriving from the French-Netherlandish architectural family of Du Ry, and, like Neumann, was an officer of Engineers. He soon had a flourishing Dublin practice. He was destined to remodel Carton for the Earl of Kildare and was the designer of the famous Dublin hospital, the Rotunda, although he died in 1751 a few months before his plans began to be put into action. Arriving in Ireland, well-versed in the tradition of Palladio, but sympathetically disposed towards the new decorative trends in France and in his native Germany, his influence quickly made itself felt.

The house was built on land bought in 1741 from an impover-

RUSSBOROUGH

JOSEPH LEESON,
1ST EARL OF MILLTOWN,
BY POMPEO BATTONI

ished M. P., James Graydon, soon after Leeson had inherited a fortune from his father who was a wealthy Dublin brewer. Leeson was a man of very considerable taste. He commissioned Count Rogone Chizzole to collect statues, paintings, porcelains, damasks etc. for the home which he was constructing in Ireland. Statues from Herculaneum, pictures that a grand duke or a king might envy, were to find their way to this house which looks out, across pasture land and an informal willow-bordered lake, towards the river Liffey and the not too distant mauve and blue Wicklow Mountains.

Russborough is twenty miles from Dublin, and two from the pleasant eighteenth-century town of Blessington. Two Englishmen, who toured Ireland in 1748, saw the work in progress, and one of them wrote, 'If we may judge of the picture by the outlines we shall when finished see a compleat beauty. Artificers from most parts of Europe are employed in this great work'.

It was built of stone from the neighbouring Golden Hill quarry. It consists of a centre and two wings, connected by semicircular colonnades of Ionic pillars, with granite mouldings and frieze, topped by a series of urns. In the colonnades are niches containing statues of Jupiter, Ceres, Hercules, Bacchus, Venus and Saturn on the left side; and of Diana, a dancing Faun, Tragedy, Comedy, Mercury and Apollo on the right.

Russborough's frontage is seven hundred feet, which is greater than that of the Würzburg Residenz. But it achieves this modestly and with the aid of the low walls which link up the wings with the two porched stable-yard gateways, on one of which is a sundial and on the other a clock.

The arrangement of the central block is simplicity itself. One mounts a wide flight of low steps, guarded by two heraldic stone lions,

below: MILLTOWN'S CONTEMPORARIES SNEERED AT HIS 'ROCOCO TEMPLE'

and passes straight into the Grand Hall, a magnificent room, out of which five other doors lead. To the left is the drawing-room, and to the right what was formerly the library and is now the dining-room, the library having been moved to a corresponding but more sequestered room on the far side of the house.

Since the Grand Hall is nearly double the depth of the two rooms which flank it, there is space for a further room on the left, the tea-room or tapestry-room, and for the well of both the main staircase and the back staircase in a corresponding position on the east side, before one reaches the entrance door of the middle of the three very beautiful rooms which fill the entire north side of the block, the music room, the Saloon and the library.

The storey above is laid out with the same ease and directness. There, both staircases emerge onto an immense carpeted lobby, which has more the air of a *grande salle* than a lobby. In the centre of it are two white pillars at either end of an oval, raised cupola, which gives light from four windows and which has decorative plaster reliefs. All round this lobby – where nothing has been allowed to intervene and spoil the calm simplicity of the architect's original conceptions – are the nine doors of the guest bedrooms, some with a spacious powder closet which was metamorphosed about the time of Edward VII into a bathroom.

Apart from its virtues of grace and symmetry the crowning splendours of Russborough are its ceilings and its mantelpieces, and the rococo murals in certain of its rooms. Richard Castle's highly-varied ceilings, sometimes coved, sometimes in rectangular compartments – the architect's favourite style – provide a series of agreeable surprises as one passes from room to room.

Each of the mantelpieces is a museum piece and it would be hard to say which is the most beautiful. They vary greatly both in design and substance. A head of Silenus in white marble may be superimposed upon a background of grey Sicilian marble. In another case the stone has been quarried in Connemara or Kilkenny. Exquisite classic heads in the purest white Parian – one of them bearing a close resemblance to the Homer at Naples, the other a possible Euripides, and each of them forming part of a hermes of coloured marble inlaid with a line of white – preside on either side of the fireplace in the Saloon. Often the centre piece is a small rectangular relief in white marble: in this case, Androcles and the Lion; elsewhere, Leda and the Swan.

The family had been prominent in public life, although in 1798 they seem to have been undeservedly suspect, probably because a certain Joseph Leeson, nephew of the then earl, was accused of sympathy with the United Irishmen, and was labelled 'the chief agitator that first seduced from their allegiance the peasantry of the County Wicklow'. The rebels occupied Russborough but treated all its art treasures with studied respect, refraining from the temptation to make national flags out of the green drugget which covered the very beautiful inlaid flooring of the Saloon on the grounds that their brogues might then 'ruin his Lordship's floor'. The soldiery who followed

SHALLOW, CURVED PORCHES FLANK THE FAÇADE

THE ENTRANCE STEPS

them, however, made the place a shambles, and the government refused all compensation for their very lengthy and highly destructive stay, and even exacted taxes for the time when they had been there.

Russborough, which for a time was in the possession of Captain Denis Daly, houses today the Beit Collection of paintings and art treasures arranged without ever impairing the atmosphere of a home, and with such taste, that at no time in its history can it have been nearer the intention of its first owner to make it a repository for beautiful things. Vermeer's *The love-letter*, Goya's superb portrait of Doña Antonia Zarate, Murillo's six paintings of the Prodigal Son (one of them recovered by Lord Dudley from the Pope) and numerous other historic pictures hang on its walls, and the niches in the walls of the Grand Hall shelter a most superb collection of bronzes and porcelain.

Monk Gibbon

RUSSBOROUGH

THE ENTRANCE HALL

A PORTRAIT OF ANTONIA ZARATE

STUCCO RELIEFS ON THE WALL OF THE STAIRCASE

osite: LEDA AND THE SWAN: DETAIL OF FIREPLACE IN THE MUSIC ROOM

243

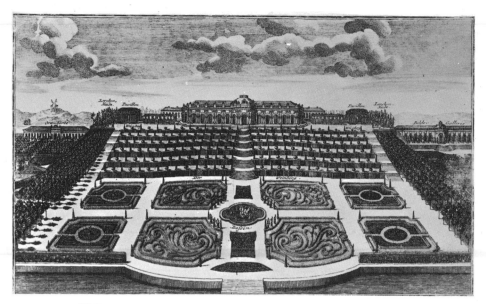

THE GARDEN FRONT SOON AFTER ITS COMPLETION

Sans Souci

A retreat for a philosopher-king

POTSDAM is a name that for some people evokes only the militarism of Prussia, but for others recalls all that is most imaginative and light-hearted in the German character. The town contains one of the earliest arms-factories in Germany, but it was an arsenal adorned with classical statues, while its garrison church carried on its exterior panoplies and crests in sculptured relief. When Frederick William I laid out the charming new Dutch quarter, he stipulated that each house should have a garret big enough to billet at least six Grenadiers; and he turned a large part of his *Lustgarten* into a training ground for his giant soldiers. Potsdam retains to this day its dual nature. Immediately recognisable as a garrison town, it is criss-crossed with avenues, punctuated by fine buildings; and among its encircling lakes and villas possessed three of the most splendid palaces in Germany, the *Stadtschloss*, the *Neues Palais*, and Sans Souci.

Frederick the Great built the last two, and much embellished the first. But it was on Sans Souci that he bestowed his greatest talents and affection. Disliking Berlin, and willing only to reside in the *Stadtschloss* during the winter months, he sought a site nearby for a summer palace, where he could work, think, and entertain, in almost monastic privacy, the few men like Voltaire who matched his own intellectual curiosity. He found it a little way outside the town on a hill then covered with oakwoods and a sprinkling of vines. The first plan for Sans Souci (the very name 'Free from cares' reveals his purpose) is dated 1745, and is in Frederick's own hand, a rough ink-

SANS SOUCI

THE CLASSICAL ENTRANCE TO A ROCOCO PALACE

A SKETCH DRAWN BY FREDERICK THE GREAT
IN 1745 TO GUIDE HIS ARCHITECTS

drawing which crudely but unmistakably delineated how a bank of terraces, curved like shallow brackets, would contour the easy gradient of the hill, and how a wide flight of steps would lead upwards through the terraces to terminate on a flat platform on which the house itself would stand. In essentials, Frederick's plan was carried out. The terraces are faced with glass-houses, themselves curved to catch the sun's rays from different angles, and above them rests, as gently as a dirigible, the low, ochre, one-storey palace which swells at its centre into a shallow dome supported by groups of superbly drunken Bacchants which extend their frolics across the whole width of the façade.

Sans Souci has three natures. The garden, like the façade of the house facing it, is a romantic variation on a classical composition. Its fountains, statuary and pavilions are today half-hidden by the hedges and huge magnolias which Frederick must have imagined, though he would never live to see, in their prime. But on the reverse side of the house, his architect, Georg Wenzelaus von Knobelsdorff, was allowed to return to the classical tradition with his great curving colonnades of Corinthian columns, pierced in the centre by a vista of a ruined folly on the top of a neighbouring hill. The visitor approaching from this direction, the true entrance front, is quite unprepared for the gentleness of the garden, or for the astounding rococo of the interior.

The pretence is maintained as far as the entrance-halls, where pairs of marble columns and classical statuary create the expected impression of a king's sumptuous domain. But on entering the first room on the south front, Frederick's library, any notion of frigidity is immediately dispelled. It is a circular room, opening directly onto the terrace, and is lined with Frederick's book-cases backed by a warm brown cedar-wood, against which wanders the leafy ormolu of its designer, Johann August Nahl. The adjoining bedroom and sitting-room, where Frederick died in an armchair in 1786, was redecorated in a Greco-German style that became fashionable soon after his death. But in the music room beyond and in the room named after Voltaire (though the philosopher fell from favour before it was ready for his occupation), the fantasy and brilliance of the rococo decoration is unequalled anywhere in Europe. The abundant use of naturalistic forms by Nahl and the brothers Johann Michael and Johann Christian Hoppenhaupt was the product of little more than two years' work, for Sans Souci was ready for the King in 1747. Metal, glass, wood, paint, marble and almost any other material that could be shaped or applied was used to transform each of these rooms into miniature stage-settings. Mirror-frames are carved into the shapes of harps, chandeliers hang like bouquets, apes perch on cornucopiae and cherubs on lattice-work, while across a ceiling strays a trellis of gold on white, overrun with vines and swept by gilded cobwebs.

Short-lived as was the rococo as a decorative style, at Sans Souci it achieved everything of which it was capable. Here was a king who made no secret of his dislike of contemporary German culture, and habitually spoke and wrote in French to his intimates, yet created with the help of German artists on German soil a palace which gave to Europe a work of art of which all Europe can be proud.

Nigel Nicolson

opposite: THE ROCOCO DETAIL OF THE MUSIC R

The palace is surprisingly light-hearted for so stern a monarch

THE NAME 'SANS SOUCI' EXPRESSED FREDERICK'S HOPES FOR PEACE

KNOBELSDORFF'S CURVING PORTICOES OF THE ENTRANCE FRON

THREE OF THE JOVIAL FIGURES THAT SUPPORT THE ARCHITRAVE

CHAIR IN WHICH FREDERICK DIED

THE KING'S DEATH-MASK

BÜRING'S CHINESE PAVILION, 1755

THE ROOM DECORATED FOR VOLTAIRE BY HOPPENHAUPT, 1753

THE CHINESE FASHION ORIGINATED IN ENGLAND

CHINESE FIGURES BY BENKERT AND HEYMÜLLER

THE GARDEN-ROOM OF THE ELECTRESS

Benrath

A marvel of delicacy and ingenuity

AN ARCHITECTURAL miracle; the perfect house for a large family of children; a residence considerably more solicitous for the comfort of its inhabitants than many of its epoch, Benrath, near Düsseldorf, in the two hundred years which have elapsed since it was built, has seen remarkably little human occupation. Karl Theodore (1724-1799), Elector Palatine, who caused Benrath to be built, had plenty of alternative accommodation – in Mannheim, in Heidelberg, in Schwetzingen nearby – and by the time Benrath was completed it had lost most of its *raison d'être*. The couple, whose initials are set over the doors of the two salons either side of its Kuppelsaal, were on terms of the coldest intimacy and only appeared on state occasions together; and the people of Munich would before long be insisting that he should live in their midst. They disliked Karl Theodore. But an Elector of Bavaria could not be allowed to live out of his realm.

It was in 1755 that he instructed Nicolas de Pigage to design a new summer palace at Benrath, to replace a much older one, a portion of which can still be seen in the woods.

Born in Lunéville in 1723, the son of an architect, Pigage studied under Emmanuel Heré and later went to the Royal Academy of Architecture in Paris and was a pupil of the famous Blondel. Then followed visits to Italy and to England, where he studied the new style of garden architecture and at one time contemplated writing a book about it. In 1749 he entered the service of Karl Theodore. He helped

BENRATH IN 1806, FROM A PAINTING BY VERNET NOW IN THE
PALAIS DE L'ÉLYSÉE, PARIS

BENRATH

KARL THEODORE

NICOLAS DE PIGAGE

CENTRE OF THE GARDEN FRONT

ENTRANCE TO THE MAIN BUILDING

with the planning of the park at Schwetzingen and the building of the ravishing little theatre; and he was responsible for many small houses in Frankfurt, Heidelberg and elsewhere.

Pigage's designs for Benrath are a marvel of delicate accuracy and ingenuity. 1795 saw extensive shiftings of soil; various subterranean canals were dug to carry water for the many fountains, as well as an underground corridor through which all food would be brought, since the main part of the Schloss was to have no kitchen on its premises. The Seven Years War saw an interruption in the work. When it was resumed, it proceeded slowly. The Elector was at Benrath in 1753, and again in 1769, as well as for other shorter periods; and the work went on slowly all the time. By 1770 it was almost finished, but the outbuildings were not completed till 1780.

Benrath reveals such architectural talent and brilliant solutions to spatial problems that it might almost be made an object lesson for members of the profession. It is disarming in its exterior simplicity; yet astounding in its internal complexity. No one seeing its flight of shallow steps leading up to what appears to be a one-storey building would suspect that as many as four storeys are concealed elsewhere, behind that façade; it only becomes evident in the two deep oval courts which hide out of sight in the centre of the building and which provided light and air for a huge domestic staff whose services were to be all too seldom requisitioned. Even the vast chimney flues, which collect smoke from far distant fireplaces by some miracle of their own, have no exit visible from the front of the Schloss.

One stands by the iris-fringed lake with its single, tiny islet on which a weeping-willow is growing, fringed by small green shrubs, to contemplate the pink frontage of the central block, with its white shutters, its bulging span of slated and windowed roof, and its circular railing above the domed centre of a building that is arranged on a completely symmetrical plan. What is there to suggest that no less than eighty rooms – many of them two-storeyed and gracious staterooms – are clustered within? Rectangular chimneys with flat tops protecting them are hidden out of sight, well behind that pediment with its sculptured cherubs and urns, its gilded clock-face and its lions from the Wittelsbach coat of arms. In spring the blossoms of the red horse-chestnuts in bloom in the woods on either side match this pink façade. Separated a little distance from it, extending forwards in a sweeping curve as though to afford protection, are the two *Kavalierflügel*, or cavalier wings. They are lower and even more modest than the central block, yet each has accommodation of eighty rooms. A study of the ground-plan reveals the symmetry and careful logic of what is really a most complex undertaking. A long, rectangular vestibule, white and a shade cold, with its marble floor and stucco reliefs by Egell of The Four Elements and The Four Seasons, is flanked on either side by an elaborate group of eight rooms together with cleverly-hidden staircases and enclosed oval courts. But it is really the prelude to a circular and domed hall, the *Kuppelsaal*.

Out of this hall opens, on either side, a *Gartensaal*, one for the Elector and one for his wife, and over each doorway is a medallion and the appropriate monogram. They are rooms for general receptions and are almost as large as the vestibule. The striking feature of the *Kuppelsaal* is its dome which is carried out as a free-spanning *calatte* with a skylight set above. There are two galleries recessed in it, one of which was used by musicians. Krahe has painted frescoes at each of these levels, so that one looks upwards past a vision of Diana and her train, through a small orifice in the centre of the fresco to the second gallery and to another recessed fresco which represents Flora and which closes the dome. The *Kuppelsaal* has a magnificent floor of patterned and polished marble, said untruthfully to have been left in a pitiable condition by the hooves of the French horses in the time of Napoleon. In any case the floor has recently been reversed and polished, and felt slippers are necessary for all who cross it.

Pigage, Dientz, Verschaffelt and Albuzio all contributed to the decoration of the rooms and there is wood-carving by Egell and von den Branden. Most of the decoration suggests a dignified retreat from the more extreme exuberance of rococo towards the classicism which was to follow. Each *Gartensaal* has a ceiling painted by Krahe— Zeus and Athene on Olympus for the Elector, Apollo and the Nine Muses for Elizabeth Amalie. Over the doorways of each room are pastoral scenes by Leitenstorffer. Of these two lovely rooms, that of the Electress, is perhaps the more pleasing.

The rooms of the separate suites adjoining these reception rooms are charming. Those on the east side were badly damaged during the war but have now been restored with considerable skill and understanding. The beautiful galleried room at the top of the house, which was the chapel, has also been restored, where the servants sat right under the roof, looking down on the celebration of the mass through windows. On the ground floor the Elector's bathroom with its ceiling of multitudinous leaves and that of the Electress with its hanging folds of plaster drapery are interesting in their suggestion of the period.

When Napoleon founded his Rhineland Duchy of Berg he put his marshal Murat at the head of it and the latter moved into residence at Benrath. Murat must have liked it, with its English and French gardens and its long stretch of placid water which leads between trees from the back of the Schloss in the direction of the Rhine; for he commissioned the French painter Vernet to make a painting of it. But Murat only remained two years. In 1808 he became King of Naples. Later he was to die at the hands of a firing squad, having badly misjudged the likely outcome of Napoleon's landing from Elba. Benrath became a Prussian possession and was occasionally used in the summer by members of the Hohenzollern family.

Monk Gibbon

STUCCO ON AN OVAL BATHROOM

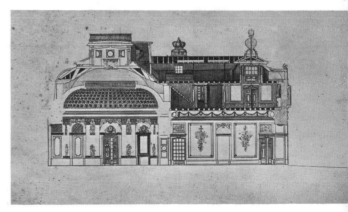

PIGAGE'S SECTIONAL DRAWING
OF THE VESTIBULE AND DOME

overleaf left: AN OVAL COURTYARD OF THE INTERIOR
right: DOME AND INNER DOME OF THE KUPPELSAAL

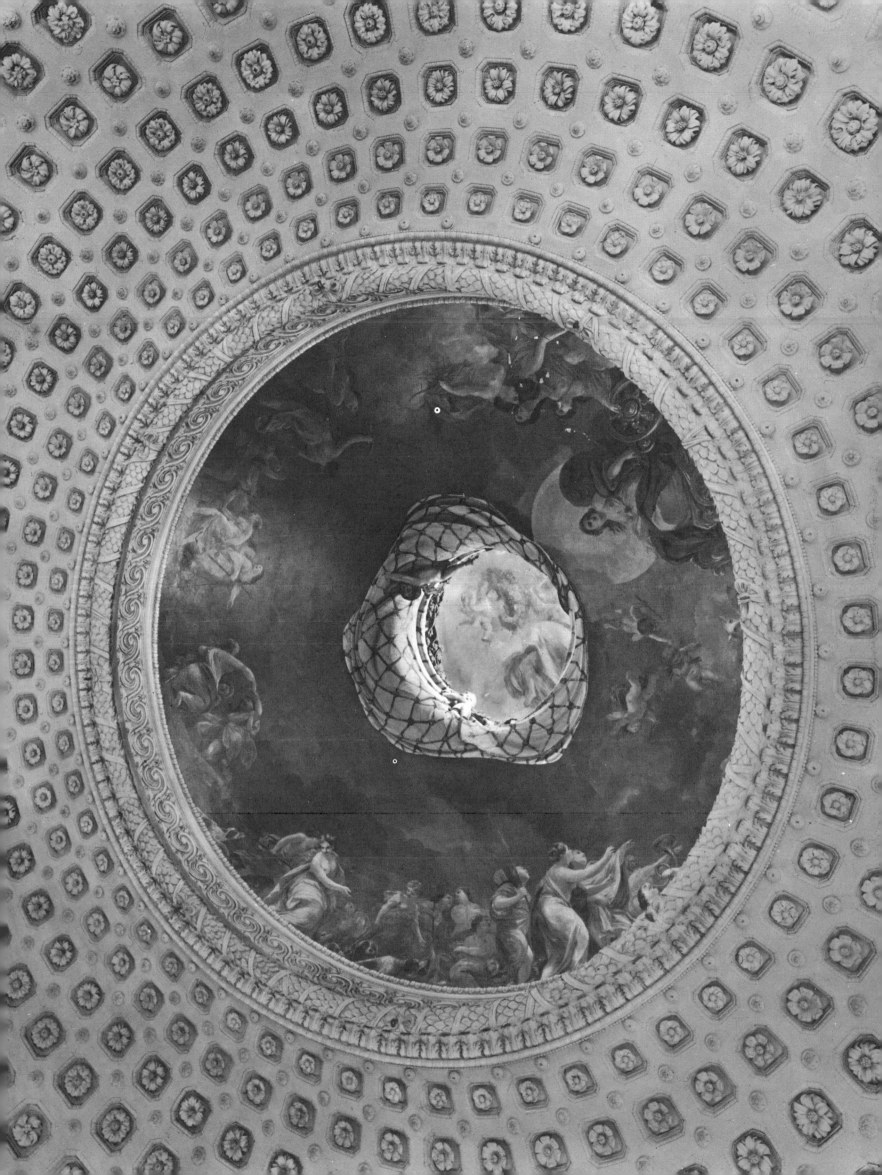

The ingenuity of Nicolas de Pigage and his decorators

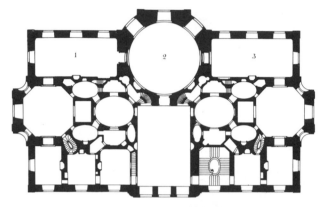

THE TWO OVALS IN THE CENTRE
ARE THE INNER COURTS

THE ELECTOR'S GARDEN-ROOM (3 ON PLAN)

THE KUPPELSAAL (2), LINKING THE TWO GARDEN-ROOMS

STUCCO IN THE VESTIBULE   PORTRAIT OF THE ELECTRESS   GILT WOOD CARVING

below: THE KUPPELSAAL

THE FORTRESS-LIKE FAÇADE CONTRASTS WITH THE ELEGANT INTERIOR

Syon House

A house transformed by Adam with imperial lavishness

ABOUT 1431 a Brigittine nunnery was moved a few miles from Twickenham to a 'more meet, healthful and salubrious' site on the Thames at Isleworth, where Syon Abbey was built. Originally one of a pair, with Sheen, it had been founded sixteen years earlier by Henry V and was the only house in the country devoted to the order founded by St Bridgit of Sweden. Shakespeare refers to it in *Henry V*:

> *I have built*
> *Two chantries, where the sad and solemn priests*
> *Sing still for Richard's soul.*

The nunnery lasted for just over a century, when it was dissolved, without undue opposition, by Henry VIII, and the Abbess was pensioned off with £ 200.

As the richest monastic house in Middlesex, Syon was a great prize after the Dissolution and fell to the Protector, Edward Seymour, Duke of Somerset. After his execution in 1552 it passed to John Dudley, Duke of Northumberland, and his wife, Lady Jane Grey, both of whom were executed in the following year. The next owner of note, Henry Percy, the 'wizard' Earl of Northumberland, was keenly and impartially interested in the exploration of North America, Dr. John Dee's experiments in magic and Shakespeare's plays (he formed a collection of the early quartos, now at Petworth). Riches and distinction were apt to attract disaster in Tudor England, and the Wizard Earl had the misfortune to be visited by Guy Fawkes on the eve of the Gunpowder Plot. Fined £ 30,000, he was unable to pay and spent fifteen years in the Tower of London.

opposite: THE ENTRANCE HALL, INSPIRED BY THE *ATRIA* OF POMP

Syon was reconstructed by Protector Somerset, improved by the Wizard Earl, and restored by his successor, who may have employed Inigo Jones on the arcaded 'cloisters', but the central courtyard and the plain, castellated exterior retain a strong flavour of their monastic origin, and the latter has scarcely changed since it was painted by Canaletto in 1752.

In 1750 it passed into the hands of the Percy heiress, Elizabeth, who was married to Sir Hugh Smithson, reputed to be the best-looking and most charming man in the kingdom. He was permitted to take the Percy name and arms, and his modest refusal of the premiership was rewarded with the Dukedom of Northumberland. His lively and amiable Duchess collected works of art, corresponded with Boswell and paid a visit to Voltaire, who presented her with a melon and a pineapple, but her grand style of life finally cost her Queen Charlotte's friendship, as the latter disapproved of the Duchess travelling with a larger retinue than the Queen's.

In 1760 Robert Adam, who had returned two years earlier from Italy, full of energy and ideas, was commissioned by the Duke and Duchess to redecorate Alnwick, their castle in Northumberland. In 1762 he started work at Syon, and by 1764 Horace Walpole reported that the house was 'becoming another Mount Palatine', though he grumbled at the new gateway and screen on the Brentford Road, 'all lace and embroidery... From Kent's mahogany we are dwindled to Adam's filigree'. Adam worked under great difficulties at Syon; he had to conform to the awkward proportions of the Jacobean rooms and was not allowed to correct the irregular floor-levels. The five staterooms, which was all that he completed, show his genius at its most daring.

The effect of the hall is overwhelmingly Roman, cool and majestic but avoiding the grandiose or pompous. The floor is of black and white marble, the walls and ceiling painted creamy white. At one end a plaster statue of the Apollo Belvedere stands below a half-dome inspired by the Pantheon; at the other a bronze version of the dying Gaul occupies the centre of a Doric screen. Four other full-scale statues, a quantity of busts and some hall-chairs with the Percy arms, complete the furnishings. The twisted columns framing two of the windows are copied from a plate by Piranesi, whom Adam knew in Rome. The *grisaille* roundels, by G. B. Cipriani, were perhaps intended to be replaced by stucco reliefs.

From here we pass to the Anteroom, which evokes, not classical antiquity, but the Rome of the High Renaissance. Twelve *verde antico* columns, dredged from the bed of the Tiber, support an entablature on which stand, as if suspended in the air, twelve gilt gods and goddesses. The walls are pale green, with blue panels decorated with gilt stucco trophies by Joseph Rose, imitated from trophies in the Palazzo Madama in Rome. A blue and gold frieze runs round the wall, two alcoves hold bronze statues of Hector and Achilles and the floor is brilliantly coloured scagliola work. This magnificent room, the most audaciously splendid of any work by Adam, was used only as a waiting room for servants.

ADAM'S DESIGN FOR THE DINING-ROOM CEILING

THE ORIGINAL DRAWING FOR THE GALLERY
(compare photograph *opposite*)

SYON HOUSE

The dining-room, with its statues in marbled niches and its medallion portraits of the Duke and Duchess, is less extraordinary. But the next room again produces an exotic and luxurious effect. This is the red drawing-room, so called from the red silk wall-hangings from the Spitalfields factory. The carpet, signed by T. Moore and dated 1769, doubtless follows a design of Adam's; the door-surrounds are of ormolu on ivory; but the most astonishing feature is the coved ceiling decorated by Angelica Kauffmann with an infinity of square and octagonal medallions in tones of blue, red and green. The effect of so many small divisions is amazing rather than beautiful, and Sir William Chambers's comment – 'a myriad skied dessert dishes' – is not wholly unjust.

Double doors, to exclude the noise of the men's conviviality over their port in the dining-room, separate the red drawing-room from the long gallery, intended for the ladies. Both the colours and the details of this room convey an effect of extreme delicacy. To conceal its awkward length Adam divided it into a series of decorative units, separated by pilasters arranged in groups of three and painted by Pergolesi at a cost of three guineas each. The walls are pale green, the pilasters and bookcases mauve, and the decoration includes marble and *stucco duro* reliefs, Italian views, a pair of distorting mirrors and a frieze of medallion portraits of members of the Percy family, among whom one observes with surprise Charlemagne. Marquetry furniture, pale green and gold chairs in the French taste and inlaid marble-topped sidetables match, both in scale and quality, the delicacy of the decoration. At either end of the gallery miniature rooms are hidden, one decorated with tropical birds, the other with a birdcage.

Adam's work at Syon ends here; he was not allowed to cover the courtyard with a dome and make it into the centre of the house, and the staterooms were completed, discreetly and without inspiration, in the nineteenth century. The house still belongs to the Duke of Northumberland—last of the great houses in and round London to remain in the possession of the original family.

Anthony Hobson

Colour-plate SYON IN THE SEVENTEENTH CENTURY BY JAN GRIFFIER

THE ARCHITRAVE OF THE DINING-ROOM

A BIRD-CAGE IN THE BOUDOIR OFF THE GALLERY

AN IVORY DOOR-PANEL OVERLAID WITH ORMOLU

ADAM'S DRAWING IN 1765 FOR A MEDALLION IN THE STAIRCASE CEILING

The astonishing richness of Syon
never degenerates into vulgarity

264

THE CEILING OF THE RED DRAWING-ROOM IS EMBELLISHED WITH PAINTED MEDALLIONS

THE ANTE-ROOM AT SYON

opposite: THE RED DRAWING-ROOM

Youssoupoff Palace

The shade of Rasputin stirs beneath these saloons

CONFOUNDING ALL traditional conceptions of haunted houses, the Youssoupoff Palace spreads its serene classical pale yellow façade boldly along the Moika flaunting a stately row of Palladian columns quite brazenly in the brisk Leningrad sunshine. The visitor to 94 Moika, however, is not deluded – he remembers tell-tale stains on the ice and unworthy excuses, and ludicrous prattle of dead dogs against the background of a cold night sky; he sees in his mind's eye a group of frightened men bearing the bound and bleeding form of a debauched monk who refused to die.

If the shade of the notorious Gregory Efimovitch Rasputin haunts the shadows of this palace, the other Youssoupoff establishments do not fall far behind in this regard. A smaller version of the Moika residence also in St Petersburg, this one in Liteinaia Street, was saddened by the mute presence, immured behind the bed, of the decaying corpse of a young revolutionary loved by the beautiful and amorous Zenaïde Ivanovna, Princess Youssoupoff, who had smuggled him out of captivity in the Swiaborg Fortress in Finland. This macabre note is struck again, this time to a stupefying degree, in the Moscow house, a vast straggling mediaeval construction with brightly checkered Muscovite roofs with a concealed tunnel leading directly into the Kremlin itself. When the present Prince's parents decided to open up this seven mile long passage, the grim record of the blind cruelty of Ivan the Terrible, the original owner of the house, stood revealed for all to shudder at; rows of crumpled skeletons were found each one chained

268

THE NEO-POMPEIAN CEILING OF THE RED DRAWING-ROOM

Lennart Olson

THE PRIVATE THEATRE

RASPUTIN IN HOSPITAL AFTER
THE ATTEMPT ON HIS LIFE

to the damp walls of a long gallery which had remained their sealed tomb since the sixteenth century.

The history of the Leningrad Palace, however, is more recent. It was a present from the Empress Catherine to her favourite Princess Tatiana Youssoupoff, one of the five nieces of the great Potemkin. The architect it not known, although most of the palaces built in St Petersburg between 1741 and 1754, when the gift was made, were the work of Rastrelli and his pupils Kwasow, Ivaninsky and Swijasew. Gratefully abandoning what can only be conjecture, we have reliably recorded testimony that Giacomo Quarenghi enlarged the building 'in the years following 1785'. The last of the great architects of Italy, as Sacheverell Sitwell has called him, was addicted to the Palladian manner and it seems certain that the splendid façade is his as well as the elegant semi-circular inner court with its colonnade leading to the garden.

Just as this work was able, one suspects, to efface all evidence of the original design, subsequent activity has successfully spoiled many of the charming effects that Quarenghi must have created, certainly as far as the interior decoration is concerned. Prince Felix Youssoupoff himself writes that 'only some of the drawings-rooms, ballrooms and galleries had retained their eighteenth-century appearance'. Andrei Alexeivitch Michailoff carried out drastic alterations in 1830 and it is probably to him that we owe the 'Russian Louis XVI' flavour

THE STAGE OF THE THEATRE, WITH PROSCENIUM PAINTED BY LIEBHARDT

Lennart Olson

of the painted neo-Pompeian ceilings echoing faintly the exquisite work of de Gault and much of the excessive Empire *pâtisserie* clinging to the walls, doors and columns.

The lovely Princess Zenaïde Youssoupoff of whom we have spoken, was clearly a woman of outstanding character – endowed, as her great-grandson has engagingly put it, with a *cuisse légère*, she finally passed away in Paris in 1897 aged one hundred. She it was who supervised the redecoration of the Moika Palace. In spite of her triumphant love-life, this lady appears to have suffered from a compulsive urge to write on walls which she sublimated by having her entwined initials incorporated in the décor of the Palace on every possible, and many impossible, occasions; no fewer than sixteen 'Y's, each tottering under the weight of a heavy crown, appear on a single Arab-inspired doorway leading to the Royal Box of the private theatre.

It is easy to imagine the glittering receptions that were held, some, we are assured, for as many as two thousand people, the vivid costumes, the flashing orders and jewels of the guests filing up the magnificent richly inlaid marble staircase, reminiscent of the Escalier de la Reine at Versailles, the sumptuous silver and gold plate, the Sèvres services bearing every variety of exotic dish to titillate the sluggish palates of a bored St Petersburg aristocracy. On these occasions supper would be served in the galleries, a foyer leading off the theatre being reserved for the Imperial family.

below: PRINCESS ZENAÏDE YOUSSOUPOFF, RE-PUTEDLY THE MOST BEAUTIFUL WOMAN IN RUSSIA, AT THE PALACE IN ABOUT 1870; AND ONE OF THE SMALLER ROOMS AT THE SAME DATE. FROM CONTEMPORARY PHO-TOGRAPHS

Lennart Olson

THE STAIRCASE, THE EMPTY SCENE OF PAST MAGNIFICENCE

The impressive chain of halls which formed the picture galleries are today stripped of canvasses and filled instead with the dreadful furniture which appears in the photographs accompanying this description; they were originally hung with valuable works now either sold or seized by the National museums, including several important Rembrandts, examples by Claude, Watteau, Boucher, Fragonard, Robert, Teniers, Ostade, de Hooch and all the approved masters of the period, not forgetting Greuze *ad nauseam*. Much of the statuary remains and the work of Canova and the French eighteenth-century sculptors was favoured above all others.

The Youssoupoffs housed in this palace their personal jewels as well as the sensational collection of precious stones reputedly the most valuable in the world. Many of their gold, enamelled and diamond-set snuff-boxes, masterpieces by Pauzié, Ador and Scharff are now in the Gold Room of the Hermitage or in collections spread over Europe.

The theatrical tradition persists in the family – it was to Price Boris Youssoupoff, chief adviser to the Empress Elizabeth, that the first Russian National Theatre owed its foundation in 1756; later under Catherine, his son Prince Nicolas was put in charge of the Imperial Theatres. The present Prince Felix, leading a simple life in Paris and devoting his time to the needy, confesses that the only time he interrupts his hermit's existence is to see a play or a ballet. It is hardly surprising, then, that one of the most important features of the palace was the private 'Louis XV' theatre where the Imperial family were frequent and honoured guests. Regretfully it must again be set down that however felicitous this may have been – and probably was – in its original form, nearly all has been transformed as a result of the rebuilding at the end of the nineteenth century by Stepanoff. With the passing of years it had a chance, even so, of fading and acquiring some sort of discipline and unity of tone allowing us to feel, at least, an agreeable nostalgia. But restoration is the fashion in the Soviet Union today and although most of it is well intentioned and some of it is excellent, enthusiasm too often transcends judgement.

The theatre has been subjected to this drastic treatment; indeed, one has the impression that some demented pastry cook has been allowed to run riot with an incontinent piping-set filled with golden icing sugar. One admirable feature remains, however, and this is the *trompe-l'œil* curtain with its celestial figures painted across the proscenium arch above the stage by the German artist Liebhardt.

What we retain in the memory of this palace on the water's edge are not the oppressive *richesses* of the ground and upper floors, but an indelible image of a black December night in 1916 and a narrow steel-lined underground room, hastily and secretly furnished in order to lure the Tsarina's holy man to his death. Here he was poisoned with cyanide of potassium, shot several times at point-blank range and repeatedly stabbed, but still did not expire until later that night when he eventually drowned alone under the ice of the Neva.

A. Kenneth Snowman

Lennart Olson

THE BALLROOM

Lennart Olson

THE ROTUNDA ON THE FIRST FLOOR

A SPHINX BELOW THE PORTICO DOS CAVALINHOS

Queluz

A rose-pink palace set in a water-garden

THE PALACE OF QUELUZ lies scarcely more than five miles from the centre of Lisbon. The new road to Sintra runs directly past its front gates. Along the old road, ribbon development – a rare phenomenon in Portugal – has brought the suburbs within earshot, though mercifully not yet within sight, for a barrier of low hills marks the limit of this modern encroachment. A fold in the ground likewise conceals the nearby railway line, so that, apart from electric lighting, the immediate vicinity contains no visual evidence of the two centuries that have elapsed since the palace was built.

Queluz has often been called the Portuguese Versailles, but its size alone precludes such a comparison. Exquisite rather than magnificent, it is a small but well developed example of Portuguese rococo, colour-washed the palest pink, with two semi-circular wings springing out from the main block onto a broad cobbled square. The outside walls are perfectly plain, all the decoration being concentrated in the window pediments which follow an irregular pattern of whorls and curlicues suggestive of metalwork or even icing-sugar. The general effect indeed – and this analogy is not intended to be pejorative – is of a very expensive birthday-cake.

The palace was built by Dom Pedro, second son of Dom João V, later husband and Regent to his own niece, the imbecile Queen Maria I. The original plan was by Mateus Vicente de Oliveira, who had

THE FORECOURT

worked under Ludovice of Ratisbon on the construction of the palace of Mafra; and later the French sculptor and architect, Jean Baptiste Robillon was called in to co-operate.

Building began in 1747 but was interrupted in 1755, the men engaged on it being needed for the reconstruction of Lisbon after the great earthquake, and only resumed in 1758. Fear of a recurrence of this disaster may have dictated the final design. At any rate, Queluz, like every other building erected near the capital after the earthquake, is constructed on a horizontal rather than a vertical plane. From the gardens, indeed, it resembles not so much a single mass as a series of separate pavilions, often of different heights but never of more than two storeys, tacked one upon another to form several low wings.

The gardens are the glory of Queluz. The great topiary parterre,

EASTERN WING OF THE PALACE FROM THE STREET

THE MAIN ENTRANCE

designed in the spirit of Le Nôtre and laid out in front of the principal rear façade, is enhanced with formal balustrades, terraces and statuary. Here in hot weather the mad Queen would sit on the edge of a fountain with her legs plunged in the water – no doubt in the very position of the two lead figures that can be seen on the edge of the Neptune fountain today. Here too, along the scented box-hedged alleyways, the eccentric William Beckford once ran races with the maids of honour of the Queen's daughter-in-law, Doña Carlota Joaquina, thereby gratifying at one and the same time his aesthetic sensibilities and inordinate love of royalty.

The feature of the parterre is the Portico dos Cavalinhos, flanked by two equestrian allegorical statues of Fame by Manuel Alves and Filipe da Costa. Below these crouch a pair of stone sphinxes of singularly unequivocal gender, with slender necks encased in pleated ruffs and with virginal bosoms visible beneath flowing draperies. This pleasing mixture of the formal and the fantastic is repeated more than once in the statuary of the gardens, where, for example, classical representations of the Rape of the Sabines and of the Death of Abel alternate with figures of almost human monkeys clothed as though for a fancy-dress ball.

Beyond the Portico dos Cavalinhos, and a grotto equipped with a cascade – the first artificial waterfall to be built near Lisbon –, a broad path leads to the lower garden and the Robillon wing. Here the romantic gives way to the severely classical. An avenue of giant magnolia

SOUTH FRONT OF THE ROBILLON WING

THE EXTERIOR OF THE BALL-ROOM

THE KING'S BEDROOM

THE BOUDOIR OF THE MAD QUEEN

trees echoes the pattern of the Doric colonnade which runs the entire length of the pavilion; and from the far corner of the balustrade, finished in 1779, three years before Robillon's death, a double staircase, which joins half-way down into a single monumental spreading flight, descends towards a Dutch canal, over a hundred yards long, lined with blue and withe *azulejo* panels depicting seascapes and other marine scenes.

This distinctively Portuguese form of decorative tilework, all too frequently suggestive of kitchens or public lavatories, is particularly well suited to these surroundings, forming a natural association with the greenery of the foliage and the movement of the water. A complex of stairways, bridges and statues marks the centre of the canal. It was from here that Lord Kinnoul, the British Ambassador to Portugal during Pombal's dictatorship, saw three splendid galleys sail past with allegorical personages on board – an example of the lavish entertainments for which the palace was then famed throughout Europe. These diversions transformed the gardens of Queluz into veritable pleasure gardens, and from the surrounding hills, where the people of Lisbon used to gather to watch the fireworks on St Peter's night, they must have looked as delicate and romantic as a miniature Japanese garden.

The interior of Queluz was gutted by fire in 1934, and among much else that perished in the flames was an apparently unique wallpaper depicting the Greek Wars of Independence, in which the figure of Lord Byron appeared among the white-kilted Evzones. The only room that survived intact is the Sala das Mangas, a wide corridor lined with *azulejo* wall panels of exotic landscapes and oriental figures in yellow, blue and mauve. The other rooms, all leading out of one another, have been successfully restored.

One of the earliest in the Sala dos Embaixadores, designed by Robillon in 1757, with a ceiling painted by Francisco de Melo, representing a royal group which includes Dom José and his Queen, Dona Maria I and Dom Pedro, David Perez, the celebrated Neapolitan who was Master of the Royal Music, and various other musicians, courtiers and ladies in waiting. The music room, built in 1759 but redesigned in 1768, and the adjoining throne room are likewise distinguished for their ceilings and both contain superb crystal chandeliers.

The Sala das Merendas, the private dining-room of Dom Pedro and succeeding Portuguese monarchs, is lined with painted panels depicting groups of eighteenth-century figures picnicking in sylvan scenes – the work of João Valentin and José Conrado Rosa, who were also responsible for the delightful mirror panels in the Queen's dressing-room, a boudoir designed as a bower, where the pergola pattern of the ceiling is repeated in the floor of various inlaid woods.

When Dom Pedro died, in 1786, the main work on the interior was completed. In 1794 the Court took up residence in the palace, but the festivities there were somewhat marred by the wild shrieks issuing from the set of rooms set aside for the Queen whose religious mania had by then developed into hopeless insanity. Her eldest living son, later King João VI, ruled the country in her place but was not to remain in Queluz for long. In 1807, to escape the imminent French invasion, the royal family fled to Brazil; and the palace was subsequently commandeered by Napoleon's victorious Marshal Junot, who undertook several improvements – notably the construction of a much-needed skylight in the so-called Dark Room, which today contains a romantic portrait of Dom João's younger son, Dom Miguel, painted in 1827 during his exile in Vienna by Giovanni Ender.

On his return from Brazil in 1821, Dom João preferred the palace of Mafra, no doubt to avoid the proximity of his fierce virago of a wife, Doña Carlota Joaquina; but it was in Queluz that he died six years later, in a fantastic little bedroom with a circular domed ceiling supported on columns of mirror glass and with walls decorated with scenes from *Don Quixote*.

None of his successors resided at Queluz. The edifice gradually fell into disrepair and weeds invaded the once-trim garden paths. In 1908, however, the palace became State property and since then an enterprising government has restored it, if not to its ancient splendour, at least to its former beauty.

Xan Fielding

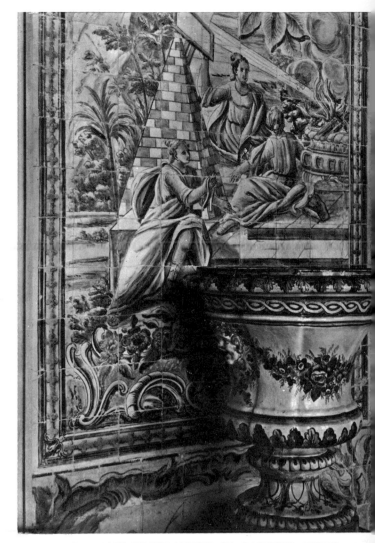

A TYPICAL WALL-DECORATION OF PAINTED TILES

The Hall of the Ambassadors, by Robillon, 1757

REFLECTIONS IN A MIRROR

THE ORIGINAL DESIGN OF THE WEST FAÇADE

Petit Trianon

The jewel of de Pompadour and Marie Antoinette

FOREIGN VISITORS TO FRANCE, accustomed to their own Buckingham Palace, their White House, their Frederiksborg, knowing Greenwich, Sans Souci or Caserta, may well say on first seeing Versailles: 'No wonder the French had a Revolution'. They will certainly understand how even the French kings found that great palace overpowering and built, first, the Grand Trianon, then the Petit Trianon, then that pathetic village, the Petit Hameau of Maria Antoinette.

To see the Trianon in psychological, historical and architectural perspective, the visitor should see the great palace first, pass by the Grand Trianon, note at its northern end the Trianon-sous-Bois and come to the Petit Trianon by way of the Pavillon Français. By following this route, he will observe the psychological changes: Louis XIV wishing to prove himself Le Roi Soleil; Louis XV wishing to have and to give pleasure; Louis XVI and Marie Antoinette wishing to prove that they were human beings as well as king and queen. The historical changes are implicit in the psychological ones: the growth of humanism. The architectural changes are more complicated, for Gabriel, who built the Petit Trianon, also built parts of the great palace.

The Gabriel of the Petit Trianon is a long way from the Gabriel of the opera at Versailles: it is surprising that the same architect could be so elaborate in one, so simple in the other. The explanation is his perfect sense of occasion, his feeling for what was demanded at the time. As a cross-reference one should look at his Place de la Concorde: a perfect concord of grandeur and simplicity.

Having seen and marvelled at the Palace of Versailles, with Le

opposite: THE WEST FAÇADE AS IT WAS BUI

PETIT TRIANON

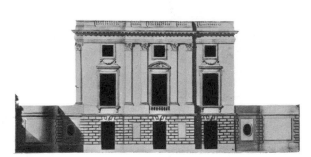

GABRIEL'S ORIGINAL DESIGNS WERE SLIGHTLY ALTERED IN EXECUTION. *top:* THE EAST FAÇADE; *top right:* THE NORTH; *and above:* THE SOUTH FAÇADE

Nôtre's tremendous achievement of turning a marsh into a landscape, one passes the Grand Trianon. One should pause at the north end of the Trianon-sous-Bois. Here is a foretaste of the change in style; elegance, simplicity, classicism. One progresses through a garden which is far less formal, and comes on the little Pavillon Français, a round room with a charming cornice frieze of farmyard animals and, off it, four tiny rooms, forming a cross.

Rounding it, the visitor sees the west front of the Petit Trianon and what a splendid piece of architecture it is! Five plain, high, unadorned windows; five even simpler, smaller ones above them; four columns; a terrace and some steps: with these few features, Gabriel has made a faultless work of art. One cannot say, 'If only it had urns on the top!', 'If only it had more carving round the windows!'.

below: THE EAST FRONT, FACING THE BOTANICAL GARDENS

above: THE NORTH FAÇADE, WHICH ORIGINALLY OVERLOOKED THE FLOWER GARDEN

below: THE SOUTH, OR ENTRANCE, FRONT

PETIT TRIANON

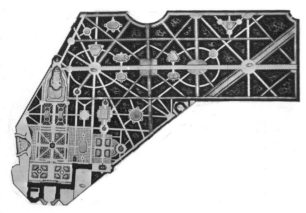

THE SURVEYOR'S PLAN FOR THE GARDEN, 1774

MARIE ANTOINETTE'S PETIT HAMEAU

THE BELVEDERE

It lacks nothing. Least of all can one say, 'If only it were larger!'.

Walking clockwise around it, one sees the north front; five tall windows with five small windows above; four columns; above these, the balustrade; below, the terrace. The even greater simplicity in line is compensated by more elaboration in the carving of the stone. The east side, compared to the others, is disappointing: but one can at least see that another side of the box has been treated differently and with even greater simplicity. Continuing clockwise, one comes, illogically perhaps, to the entrance, and then any doubts about Gabriel's genius and invention are dispelled. The walls of the little court-yard lead up to a simple ground floor; on this solid support stand five tall windows, five smaller ones above, four columns and the balustrade: the same wall-space, the same fenestration but a completely different variation on the same theme. What Mozart could do in music, Gabriel has done in stone.

Though the Petit Trianon is normally associated with Maria Antoinette, it was, in fact, the brain-child of Louis XV and Madame de Pompadour. When he became interested in botanical gardening, he extended his plans beyond the Grand Trianon. In 1750 he commissioned Gabriel to build there the *Salon de compagnie et de jeu* or *Salon de conversations et de musique*, now known as the Pavillon Français. The building of the Petit Trianon was begun for Madame de Pompadour in 1760, but, partly because of lack of money, partly owing to her death, it was not finished until 1770. It then became, in theory rather than in practice, a place of retreat for Louis XV and Madame du Barry. Not, however, until the Petit Trianon was given to Marie Antoinette did it really begin to have a life of its own. From the time of Louis-Philippe, it has been the policy of successive governments to restore to the Petit Trianon the furniture and objects which Marie Antoinette had placed there: Louis Philippe went so far as to put her monogram into the grand staircase which leads from the little entrance hall to the main rooms on the first floor.

The stairs lie just inside the entrance. The stair-well, except for some Italianate swags, is severely classical. Beyond a small ante-room lies the dining-room. In the floor one can still see where the dining-room table came up, fully-loaded, from the kitchen below, so that the company could serve themselves, without being waited on by servants. This room has an exquisite Louis XIV fireplace; the *boiseries* are fine but have been painted (they must have been either unpainted or painted white and gold – or, possibly green and gold). There is a little room beyond, museum-like and unlived-in; then a charming little salon with some fine furniture, including a superb Reisener table. One goes through a sad little bathroom into Marie Antoinette's bedroom with, among other things, a Jacob sideboard, and looks into Louis XVI's bedroom beyond. A little boudoir, decorated by Mique, and that is all. The top floor, invisible from the outside, contains the apartments of the ladies-in-waiting.

In spite of the efforts of Louis-Philippe and later ages, there is little feeling of Marie Antoinette in the Petit Trianon itself. Marvellously beautiful as the outside is, the inside is merely a museum.

THE PAVILLON FRANÇAIS

The credit for the building most go to Madame de Pompadour and Gabriel. Where Marie Antoinette has left her mark is on the surroundings. Ian Dunlop, in his admirable book on Versailles quotes de Croy: 'I thought I must be mad or dreaming. Never have two acres of land so completely changed their form, nor cost so much money'. Where Louis XV had had his hot-houses, Marie Antoinette had erected a landscape of hills, a lake, a grotto designed by Hubert Robert and a cascade. Mique, her architect, had designed a theatre, a *Temple d'Amour*, a Belvedere (with exquisite panels by Le Riche on the walls and a ceiling by Lagrenée). Reacting against the classical landscaping of Le Nôtre, she made a garden in the Anglo-Chinese manner. Going even further, topographically and romantically, she built her Petit Hameau, the little half-timbered village of cottages, dairy, and Breton tower. The influence of d'Urfé, Rousseau, Hubert Robert, the romanticisation of the simple life, caused her to go too far. The Palace of Versailles may have been grand to the point of vulgarity: Marie Antoinette's false simplicity achieved vulgarity of another kind. She should have rested content with the Petit Trianon: there she already had a masterpiece of simplicity, elegance and good taste.

Robin McDouall

ON THE TERRACE OF THE BELVEDERE

287

left: MADAME DE POMPADOUR BY BOUCHER
right: MARIE ANTOINETTE BY KOCHARSKI

A DOORWAY FROM THE DINING-ROOM TO AN ADJOINING SALOON

these small rooms

THE QUEEN'S EFFIGY SURVEYS HER BOUDOIR

MARIE ANTOINETTE'S BEDROOM

above: THE MUSIC ROOM

left: THE STAIRCASE IS SIMPLE
BY THE STANDARDS OF VERSAILLES

Arbury Hall

Tudor in origin, gothicized in the 18th century

THE ROCOCO TASTE which spread with such verve across Europe in the first half of the eighteenth century found many curious forms of expression. It took for its gay purposes not only silver *épergnes*, shell grottoes, and bell-hung pagodas, but the phoenix and the monkey; indeed the porcelain *singeries* of Meissen and Fürstenberg are among its most delightful productions. Though the taste reached England later than the Continent, it assumed in this northern setting, where it was said by 1740 'to be the fashionable distemper', the most arbitrary of its manifestations, laying even the architecture of the Middle Ages under tribute. The result was eighteenth-century Gothick of which Arbury Hall is the supreme example.

The Gothick, associated with such amateurs and architects as Walpole, Batty Langley, and Sanderson Miller, bore the most superficial relation to true Gothic, from which on paper it is conveniently distinguished by a final 'k'; yet in a number of English buildings, such as the hall at Lacock Abbey, Hartwell church, Strawberry Hill, and, above all, Arbury, it resulted in architecture that was lively and endearing, and it well expressed the essential spirit of rococo.

The Newdegates, the present owners of Arbury, have lived there since the sixteenth century, and it was their Elizabethan mansion that the 5th baronet, Sir Roger Newdigate (the original spelling of the name), began to gothicize in 1750. His portrait by Devis, which hangs at Arbury, endows him with character, a domed forehead, and

opposite: CEILING OF THE BAY-WINDOW IN THE SALO

ARBURY HALL

SIR ROGER NEWDIGATE BY DEVIS

DESIGN FOR A STABLE DOOR BY WREN

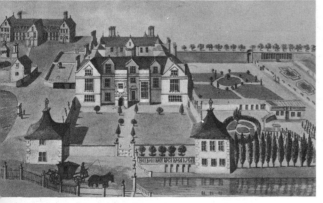

DROWING OF THE TUDOR
HOUSE BY HENRY BEIGHTON, 1708

below: SIR ROGER'S DIARY OF 1761
SHOWS THAT KEENE'S FAN-VAULT-
ING WAS INSPIRED BY THE HENRY
VII CHAPEL AT WESTMINSTER ABBEY

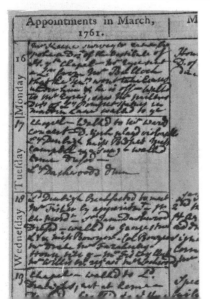

a benevolent yet melancholy cast of countenance relieved by an expression of ironic humour. Inheriting Arbury as a boy, he was its
master for seventy-two years; for thirty years he was Member of
Parliament for Oxford; and throughout his life, as befitted an eighteenth-century gentleman, he was scholar and dilettante. Though his
intelligence and his virtue, in the character of Sir Christopher Chev-
erel, were later portrayed by George Eliot, who was brought up on
the Arbury estate, his most lasting memorials are the Newdigate verse
prize which he founded at Oxford, and the charm of the house which
he transformed and which has remained unaltered since his death.

The transformation was a long one, lasting several decades, and
several architects were employed, among them probably Sanderson
Miller, whose seat was not far off at Radway, and certainly Robert Keene, Surveyor of Westminster Abbey, and Couchman, a local
Warwickshire architect. In the circumstances the unity of feeling that
informs Sir Roger's work is surprising. Though he was over eighty
when the last fragile cusp and crocket were executed, there are few
suites of rooms more of a mood, more winningly and consistently
light-hearted than his stuccoed apartments.

The delight of Arbury is missed if the visitor judges it in terms
of conventional Gothic. He will be as censorious as were the prac-
titioners of the 'correct' Gothic Revival. Arbury is not related to the
exaltations and certainties of mediaeval building but to the rococo
elegance of Bow porcelain or the more audacious designs published
by Chippendale. The suite of 'Chippendale' chairs in the Long Gallery is a better key to the understanding of Sir Roger's ornament
than all the cathedrals of northern Europe. The essential forms
of Gothic were dictated by function. At Arbury the arches, the fan
vaults, the pendants, the fluted pillars, are pure decoration. Supporting nothing, their only purpose is to please, yet for reasons no
doubt connected with the lingering prestige of Perpendicular, that
peculiarly English style, pleasure is achieved by a vivacious use of
Gothic elements. Chamfers, ogees, trefoil crestings, and filigree tracery are as a gay as rocaille, and serious ecclesiastical motifs are induced to play a role associated with the symbols of the arts, the
chase, and the boudoir. The levity of the undertaking is half its charm.

Arbury is best seen from across the lake and landscape which
Sir Roger laid out in the picturesque manner, a manner which itself
owed much initially to the rococo spirit. From this viewpoint, the south
front with its pinnacles and battlements, its traceried windows, its
projecting bays, its deep recessions and shadows, creates much of the
sense of busy movement that Sir Roger must have intended. But stone
is not the ideal medium for the expression of a rococo taste, and
the south front is too strictly symmetrical to convey its light-hearted
message. The exterior of Arbury is perhaps a little stilted, a little
unconvincing. The interior is the thing. Here a succession of enchanting Gothick rooms occupy the east and south fronts, and are linked
by the vaulted corridor, known as 'The Cloisters', which Sir Roger
inserted in the quadrangle of the old Elizabethan house.

In these rooms the dominant colours are white, or white and gold, and with their ribs, bosses, and stalactite pendants, the rooms seem, according to one's mood, shrines fantastically carved in chalk, or celestial confectionery, the work of some inspired Escoffier. George Eliot was reminded of 'petrified lacework'. The sequence proceeds through smaller apartments to the Saloon, whose fan-vaulted ceiling of extraordinary elaboration is derived from Henry VII's chapel at Westminster, and whose semi-circular bay window is perhaps the most original example of Gothick glazing in the country. The drawing-room that adjoins, with a splendid collection of 'Red Anchor' Chelsea china, whose exotic birds find here their appropriate setting, has a groined and barreled ceiling and full-length portraits framed in the Gothick wall-work. Lastly, a logical culmination, come the dining-room and library.

The dining-room, occupying the site of the Elizabethan hall, is an extraordinary *tour de force* in its successful marriage of apparently discordant elements. The framework with its sumptuous fan-vaulting and its mullioned windows in their long columned embrasure, is firmly Gothick, yet in niches on the walls under elaborate Gothick canopies are versions of well-known classical statues, and the walls themselves are closely hung with Elizabethan and Jacobean portraits. Cupid and Psyche are as strangely at home as Queen Elizabeth in lace ruff and jewelled stomacher, or Mary Fitton (sister-in-law of an early Newdigate) whose beauty is most compelling in this curious setting.

The library achieves another happy blend of classical and rococo elements. Above the elaborate Gothick bookcases with arched tops is a frieze incorporating horses, swans, and *fleurs de lys*. This prepares eye and imagination for the transition to the shallow barrel-vaulted ceiling painted wholly in the classical manner with medallions and arabesques. But the striking beauty of the room is its colour. Through the three windows in the south bay, light explores the Gothick detail of white bookcases, the gilded ceiling, and the surfaces of old leather bindings that seem as soft as velvet. The effect, unusually harmonious, is not of plaster, paint, and books, but of ivory, gold and amber.

In these Gothick rooms, and adding much to their interest, is harboured the history of four hundred years, and the accumulations of successive generations of Newdigates. The series of family portraits, which includes a work by Gilbert Stuart, the painter of George Washington, is almost comparable in its completeness to the great collections at Gorhambury, Burghley, or Woburn. The furniture is no less remarkable. Its range includes pieces used by the Duke of Suffolk before his execution in 1554, Archbishop Laud's cabinet, the rich marquetry of the late seventeenth century, Louis XV commodes, Georgian mahogany, and the polite satinwood that was fashionable when Sir Robert was an old man. Much of the attraction of Arbury is due to these accretions of time and taste.

Time has also left the imprint of the sixteenth and seventeenth centuries. Sir Roger's Gothick revolution was incomplete in the Long Gallery, where the splendid Elizabethan fireplace and overmantel survive, and in the Chapel on the ground floor. The latter, conceived by Sir Roger's grandfather, is an almost untouched example of the decoration of the time of Charles II. The powerful plaster work, with

THE STABLES

WROUGHT-IRON GATES TO THE STABLE COURTYARD

WINDOW OF THE SALOON FROM THE OUTSIDE AND INSIDE

THE LIBRARY

opposite: THE DRAWING-ROOM

its plump garlands of fruit and flowers, its flourishing acanthus, is the work of Edward Martin, a London plasterer. Its juxtaposition to the mid-eighteenth-century rooms concisely points the change in taste from the baroque to the rococo.

A few years earlier than the Chapel are the stables, immense yet gracious buildings characteristic of an age that housed its horses almost as splendidly as their owners. The stables are of weathered red brick with stone-mullioned windows, and Sir Christopher Wren made several designs for the central porch. It is set in one of three bays that are surmounted by curved gables of a type more usual in East Anglia or the Netherlands than in Warwickshire.

Stables, Chapel, Long Gallery, furniture and pictures, give Arbury its fourth dimension, an extension in time, and provide the long perspective against which Sir Roger's achievement is set.

Robin Fedden

left: THE DRAWING-ROOM FIREPLACE 295

THE DINING-ROOM WINDOWS

FIREPLACE IN THE DINING-ROOM

DETAIL OF THE FIREPLACE

An ecclesiastical Gothick imposed on the architecture of several centuries

THE CHAPEL, UNALTERED SINCE CHARLES II

left: A SMALL SITTING-ROOM

A 1780 SKETCH OF THE GARDEN FAÇADE

Hôtel d'Hane-Steenhuyse

The King's retreat during the Hundred Days

ON 5 MARCH 1815, Napoleon landed from Elba on the coast of Provence. On the 18th, Maréchal Ney went over to the side of his former Emperor, and Louis XVIII, abandoned by all but a few of his courtiers, decided to fly from the Tuileries. He took the road to Lille with only a vague idea of his final destination. Some advised him to make for England, but he was reluctant to leave the mainland of Europe. Others spoke of the friends that he was sure to find in Belgium. Eventually, alarmed by the news of Napoleon's success and discouraged by the hesitation of William I of Holland to bid him welcome in Brussels, Louis XVIII decided to make his way to Ghent. He recalled, no doubt, that when he was nothing but the Comte de Provence, he had been very well received by a charming aristocrat of that town, the Comte d'Hane-Steenhuyse. After an exhausting journey, the King reached Ghent and called on his former host, who received him with great cordiality. He stayed there exactly a hundred days, gathering round him a small court, and receiving the emissaries of all the Governments of Europe.

The Hotel d'Hane-Steenhuyse, which had been famous since the Middle Ages, is situated in the very centre of the town and in its busiest street. In 1698 the original house came into the hands of the family that still owns it. Jean-Baptiste d'Hane, the Comte de Nieulandt and Lisbeke, acquired the property in that year, but his successors, Comte Emmanuel-Ignace d'Hane (1702-1771) and his son, Comte Pierre-Emmanuel (1726-1786), pulled down the mediaeval house and

opposite: THE GARDEN FRONT AT THE PRESENT D

HOTEL D'HANE-STEENHUYSE

A PAVILION ADJOINING THE GARDEN FAÇADE

erected in its place the spendid building that we see today. They employed as their architects David 't Kint, who built the façade on the street in the style of Louis XV, and Dewez, who in 1773 designed the garden-front with its elegant window.

The French and Italians who were invited to decorate the interior made it as gay as it was sumptuous. On the ground floor, completed in 1781, there is a suite of rooms of delightful elegance. Of these the most remarkable is the Italian room, or ballroom, which rises to the full height of the house. On the level of the first floor a balcony runs round the entire room, and the floor, which took five years to construct, the work of François and Henri Feilt of Paris, is a marvellous achievement of marquetry in six types of precious wood. This was the room where Louis XVIII amused himself with his larger dinner-parties and concerts, but for his more intimate gatherings, he used the green saloon, and it is said that the people of Ghent, glancing through the windows as they passed by the house, would see him preparing to eat, as hors d'œuvres, twelve dozen oysters. The Salon Vert is embellished with wood-carvings framing superb Gobelin tapestries, and the great Savonnerie carpet is of the same date as the décor.

The Salon des Saisons, or little dining-room, is named after the wall-panels by Van Reyschoot depicting members of the contemporary aristocracy of Ghent in the countryside and at home. The artist, who also executed the ceiling-paintings in the Italian room, was obviously a man who enjoyed teasing his patrons, for in one of the panels he has shown the overturning of a lady's carriage, an incident which had caused a considerable stir in Ghent at the time, and the scene is observed from a window by a young abbot, whose delight is very evident on his face. The sense of propriety of a descendant of the Comte d'Hane caused him to have the figure of the priest changed into that of a young man.

THE COMTE D'HANE
(1702-1771)

THREE FREQUENT VISITORS TO THE HOUSE DURING THE HUNDRED DAYS
left: THE DUKE OF WELLINGTON. *centre:* CHATEAUBRIAND. *right:* LE DUC DE BERRY

THE BALLROOM CEILING, BY PIERRE NORBERT VAN REYSSCHOOT

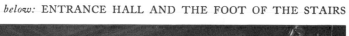

below: ENTRANCE HALL AND THE FOOT OF THE STAIRS

THE SALLE À L'ITALIENNE, OR BALLROOM

LANDSCAPE BY VAN REYSSCHOOT
IN THE SALON DES SAISONS

THE ROOM IN WHICH LOUIS XVIII SLEPT AND WORKED

below: THE SALON VERT

The other rooms in the house, including that which the King used both as his study and bedroom, and a room on the first floor with wall-paper made of Chinese rice-paper, said to have been imported by the East India Company in the eighteenth century, have created for the Hotel d'Hane Steenhuyse a reputation which is almost unequalled among the Belgian private houses of its period. Until 1905 the house remained in private occupation, and the present owners were born there. But when their careers took them to Brussels, and they had no further links with Ghent, they closed the house, and reopened it as a Museum in 1947. The public can now walk through the rooms which saw Jérome Alexander I of Russia, William I of Holland, Talleyrand, and the jovial monarch, Louis XVIII, whose name, more than any other visitor's, will always be associated with these beautiful saloons adorned by many of the finest artists of the day, working for enlightened patrons whose taste has survived as their epitaph.

Baudouin de Bousies Borluut

opposite: THE KING'S DESK SURVIVES IN THE ROOM WHICH HE OCCUPI

THE BATHING-PAVILION. DETAIL FROM A PAINTING BY BELLOTTO

Lazienki

The island-palace of the last King of Poland

AT THE END OF THE seventeenth century the traveller who approached the capital of Poland from the south and passed before the imposing castle, centre of the Ujazdów estate which dominated the vast gardens sloping towards the Vistula, could see the cupolas of a small picturesque building down below among the trees. This was the Pavilion of the Baths, the core of the existing Lazienki Palace.

At that period the estate was owned by Prince Stanislaus Lubomirski, a most powerful statesman, as well as being poet, philosopher and man-of-letters. A patron of the arts, he embellished the Pavilion of the Baths, which was probably erected during the third quarter of the century by one of his predecessors. His favourite artist, a Dutchman, Tilman van Gameren, Polish by adoption and the most famous exponent of baroque architecture in Poland, had a hand in this work. The Pavilion of the Baths ('Lazienki' in Polish) included a large rotunda with fountains in the 'grotesque' manner, bathrooms and rest-chambers, richly adorned with stucco, statues and pictures. Externally the building offered a sober aspect, relieved solely by the three cupolas, the central one of which corresponded to the rotunda.

The estate was bought in 1764 by Stanislaus Augustus Poniatowski, a noble who was already sure of his accession of the throne, which took place that same year. The last king of Poland proposed to set up his country seat there. With this in mind, he began by reconstructing the Castle of Ujazdów on the hill, a project which he soon abandoned, concentrating all his efforts on the Pavilion of the Baths which he decided to convert into a villa-residence. This became his favourite task and preoccupation. The hapless king, weak states-

opposite: THE COLONNADED BRID

LAZIENKI

KING STANISLAUS AUGUSTUS PONIATOWSKI
BY BACCIARELLI

Edward Hartwig

SOUTH FRONT OF THE PALACE

Edward Hartwig

THE MORE SEVERE NORTHERN FRONT

man though he was, proved himself an undisputed sovereign in the realm of culture and the arts and one of the most illustrious patrons in Europe. He gathered a group of architects, sculptors, painters and skilled craftsmen, Italians for the most part, round him at his court at Warsaw. He entrusted the reconstruction of the Pavilion of the Baths to the First Architect of the King, Domenico Merlini. The whole scheme was under the supervision of the Master of the Court Buildings, the painter Marcello Bacciarelli, who carried out the major part of the painted decoration.

Following unimportant modifications in the Pavilion effected between 1772 and 1777, the main reconstruction was embarked on in 1784. The present south façade was built onto the old edifice at this time. Between 1788 and 1793 the old Pavilion of the Baths was completely encompassed – sides and roofs – by new parts, with their interiors, which were added to the existing rooms, the arrangement of which was also partially transformed. The neo-classical style predominated on the exterior as in the interior where parts of the previous baroque décor were nevertheless retained – a handsome gesture on the part of a generous conqueror to an enemy who had already exhausted his defence forces. Thus the finest specimen of neo-classicism in Poland came into being; it was at the same time an expression of the efflorescence of that style there during the age of Enlightenment and one of the most attractive examples of the idiom in Europe. The Lazienki Palace is a beautiful specimen of architecture with its clearly defined volumes and light walls. The light sections are ingeniously contrasted with those in shadow. The belvedere, an unusual motif and one that lends a touch of originality to the palace, closes the ensemble at the top like a elegant classical flourish.

The chief aesthetic merit of the palace lies in its relation to the grounds. The south façade, with its portico-niche, makes an inviting entrance to the inside of the building. Its terrace is embellished with statues sloping gently down to the pond formed by the canal waters. The galleries form an extension of the palace beyond the island on both sides – towards the flanking pavilions which merge into the trees of the park. We are unaware of any feeling of dissonance as our glance shifts from natural setting to architecture, and the sunlit volumes of the palace seem to constitute as much an integral part of the garden as the canal waters, the brown gravel of the avenues and the green foliage under the blue sky. The more restrained north façade, with its projecting porch surmounted with a pediment, falls steeply away towards the water in a flight of steps.

Nor are the interiors of the Lazienki Palace any less interesting from the point of view of the development of neo-classical architecture in Europe. The rectangular ballroom, simple in its general plan, has vast wall-surfaces, some smooth, some elegantly decorated in white stucco, interrupted by panels in warm red and brown tones, adorned with grotesques so much in vogue at that period, the work of Jean Plersch. A refinement and rational discipline, very French in inspiration, are much in evidence in this room for which another court architect, Jean-Baptiste Kammsetzer, was probably responsible. We owe the architectonic element in other rooms to the more exuberant Merlini with his greater liking for opulent effects. He allotted huge surfaces in the so-called Solomon Room to paintings of biblical and allegorical subjects by Bacciarelli.

It is impossible to imagine the 'Palace on the Water' without its surrounding park. The garden was replanned and enlarged during the reign of Stanislaus Augustus in the English Romantic style, so much in favour at that time. It possesses a great deal of charm at every season of the year. The king commissioned the building of some pavilions, mostly by Merlini, between 1774 and 1793: the so-called 'White House', the small and attractive Myslewice Palace with its wings in horse-shoe form, the Orangerie linked to a theatre with a superb decoration painted by Plersch, the Amphitheatre – open to the sky in the classical tradition, with a stage separated from the audience by an arm of the canal – and guard-houses.

The Palace was the work of the last years of the reign of Stanislaus Augustus. The king was fond of retiring to it and leaving behind the affairs of state which were rapidly degenerating. There he did his work and, on occasion, gave grand receptions and, frequently, more intimate ones. Of the latter the Thursday dinner-parties, when he talked with writers and scholars, became celebrated for their conversational brilliance. He loved to contemplate the paintings in his gallery which he intended to enrich through the purchase of a collection specially made for him in London. In the end he was unable to pay for it, and it become the nucleus of the Dulwich Gallery.

The interior of the palace had not been completed when the king failed in his political duties and his reign collapsed. He was compelled to abdicate and left Warsaw. The palace soon shared the tragic fate of the Polish nation. At the beginning of the nineteenth century it became the private residence of the Czars of Russia, which it remained up to 1918, when in the newly independent Poland, its custodian, the State, threw it open to the public.

This precious gem of European art remained intact for some time during the last war. During the siege of 1939 and the German occupation, it escaped the destruction which befell the capital. It was likewise spared during the large-scale destruction of Warsaw at the time of the insurrection of 1944 and the months which followed. But when at the end of the year 1944, Hitler's troops blew up all the distinguished buildings which still remained intact, the tragic hour also struck for the Lazienki Palace. Two hundred holes were bored for dynamite in the walls of the fine Rotunda and adjacent rooms; but, as the launching of a combined Soviet and Polish offensive left the Germans no time to insert the charges, they set fire to the interior.

After the liberation the Polish government began the entire reconstruction of the palace with the aim of restoring it, externally and internally, to its original appearance. This long task is nearing completion. The finest rooms have already been restored to their former splendour. It is a dependency of the National Museum of Warsaw and has recently been opened to the public.

Stefan Kozakiewicz

Edward Hartwig

SCULPTURAL DETAIL OF THE EXTERIOR

Edward Hartwig

THE STAGE OF THE OUTDOOR THEATRE

Edward Hartwig

THE 'WHITE HOUSE', A PAVILION IN THE PARK

THE SOLOMON ROOM, WITH BIBLICAL PAINTINGS BY BACCIARELLI

AN ANTE-CHAMBER IN THE RECONSTRUCTED PALACE

CERBERUS CHAINED IN THE BALL-ROOM

The special feature of the interior is its sculpture and painting

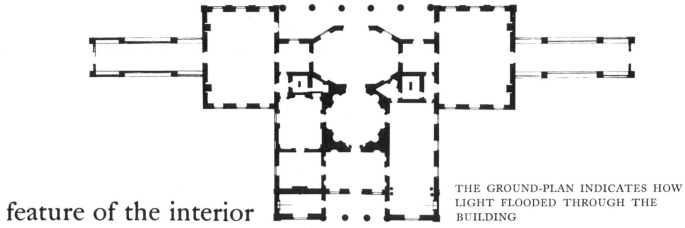

THE GROUND-PLAN INDICATES HOW LIGHT FLOODED THROUGH THE BUILDING

below: THE BALL-ROOM IS VERY FRENCH IN INSPIRATION

LAZIENKI

ONE OF THE SEVENTEENTH-CEN-
TURY ROOMS OF THE ORIGINAL
BATHING-PAVILION, LINED WITH
DUTCH TILES

A NINETEENTH CENTURY VIEW OF THE HOUSE

Casita del Labrador

'A little corner of France beside the Tagus'

ARANJUEZ IS A MIRACLE. Thirty miles south of Madrid it is a green oasis on the River Tagus. Everywhere else in New Castile is dry, yellow and parched. But in Aranjuez, there are green lawns, fountains, light breezes, and in the summer its famous strawberries seem huge and rich like lotus fruit. It was the natural place for the Spanish monarchs to have their summer palace as they had, with little interruption, since the late fifteenth century, when the mediaeval owners of the town, the knightly order of the Masters of Santiago handed it over, reluctantly, to the Catholic kings, Ferdinand and Isabella. The existing Royal Palace was built in the mid-eighteenth century by Philip V and his son Ferdinand VI, partly at least in imitation of their French cousins' magnificence at Versailles. And at the bottom of the royal gardens, along the Tagus, there is the Casita del Labrador, the neo-classical 'Labourer's Cottage' built for Charles IV and Maria Luisa, those two strange rulers whose fantastic faces stare out forever, with their children, from their brilliantly insulting portraits by Goya.

The Casita del Labrador was no doubt built with the conscious recollection of Trianon at Versailles in the mind of the architect, Isidro González Velázquez, who worked on the house between 1792 and 1803. The site chosen was actually that of a real labourer's cottage, some of whose foundations are still visible in the cellars of the present house. This is built in the form of a three-storeyed central block, with two wings, themselves divided by a courtyard and united at their

extremity by railings. The courtyard, as customary in neo-classical buildings of this type, is surrounded by twenty marble busts and statues, all being copies of a classic model, most being Roman emperors. These stand out against the pink and white brick of the Casita del Labrador itself, and the lush green of the woods which closely approach the house.

Inside, the principal and first floor is now alone properly maintained. This is reached by means of a sumptuous principal staircase, with marble steps and lined jade pillars. This leads to a suite of eighteen rooms whose principal characteristic is the collection of tapestries from the Fábrica del Buen Retiro, of furniture and, among other *objets d'art*, of clocks ('How can I be expected to rule an empire', complained the idiotic and displeasing monarch Ferdinand VII, prowling about these marble rooms, 'when I cannot get all my clocks to keep the right time?'). The most splendid rooms are those associated with Queen Maria Luisa, in particular her drawing-room with its

THE ENTRANCE FRONT

SKETCH FOR THE FAÇADE BY ISIDORO GONZALES VELAZQUEZ, 1803

magnificent tapestry and the fine baroque ceiling of the four seasons painted by the Valencian artist, Maella. A specially curious clock here is decorated by a representation of Copernicus' planetary system. Four fine Sèvres bowls recall a gift to Maria Luisa by Napoleon. This room leads into the superb *Gabinete de Platino*, a room heavily encrusted with gold, bronze and platinum, carried out with much 'Pompeian' imitations – as was inevitable at that period of the development of European taste. (There is one entire Pompeian room, full of copies of Roman heads.) The walls are additionally adorned by small views of Italian cities: Florence, Venice, Naples; while from the ceiling hangs a great chandelier, a present of Pope Gregory XVI to Ferdinand VII. Opening off this splendid piece of extravagance, there is the royal bathroom, also lavishly decorated in a Pompeian style, but never alas used: for there do not seem to have been any occasions when the Royal Family ever stayed the night at the Casita del Labrador. They only used it as a kind of adult day-nursery, where Maria Luisa might meet her absurd Godoy, the Prince of Peace, in slightly less formal circumstances than was inevitable at the big palace nearer the town.

The most touching part of this jewelled house is perhaps the elegant but severely functional service staircase. On its walls, the painter Zacarias González Velázquez (brother of the architect) has depicted a brilliant series of dancing portraits, one of his own son, another of Maria Luisa's hair-dresser, a third of Charles IV's barber. Other servants follow, half erased by time, but full of movement, gaiety and gravity, lasting expressions of that other Spain so rich in character but so little understood by the cold, mad, royal persons upstairs whom they had to serve.

Hugh Thomas

CHARLES IV AND QUEEN MARIA LUISA BY GOYA

THE SMALL STAIRCASE, WITH A SELF-PORTRAIT BY ZACARIAS VELAZQUEZ

The Casita del Labrador is a splendid flourish at the end of the 18th century

opposite: THE DECORATION OF THE DINING-ROOM

THE BILLIARD-ROOM

A PERSPECTIVE THROUGH THREE SMALL ROOMS

THE SALA CORUNNA

Exquisite care
was lavished on every corner
of the little palace

opposite: CEILING OF THE SALA CORUNNA

Acknowledgements

The Editor and Publishers wish to thank the owners of
the houses illustrated in this book, and those who
provided the additional illustrations (portraits, prints,
plans etc.) listed below. The owner's name follows
the name of each house. The illustrations are identified
by the page on which they appear, followed by an
abbreviated description of the illustration where necessary.

INTRODUCTION: *E. Boudot-Lamotte*, 8 (S. Giorgio, P. Medici), 9 (Mantua), 10 (Badoer), 11 (Gamberaia, Anet, d'O), 12 (Balleroy, Sassy), 13 (Rezzonico, Strà, Rotonda), 14 (Vienna), 17 (P. Michel). *Mansell Collection*, 9 (P. Strozzi, Pienza), 10 (Cintra, Boboli), 11 (Heidelberg) 14 (Hampton Court, C. Howard). *Phot. Karquel*, 9 (Chenonceaux). *Spanish National Tourist Office*, 10 (Guadalajara). *Section Touristique du Château de Beloeil*, 13, (Beloeil). *Netherlands Information Bureau*, 14, (Mauritshuis). *National Travel Assoc. of Denmark*, 15 (Clausholm). *Ryksvoorlichtingsdinst*, 15 (Huys ten Bosch). *British Museum*, 15 (Potsdam). *K. L. M.*, 15 (Middachten). *United States Information Service*, 16 (Mt. Vernon, Monticello). *C. T. K.*, 17 (Krummau)

THE DUCAL PALACE, URBINO: Gallerie delle Marche. *Alinari*, 21 (both portraits). *Gallerie delle Marche*, 21 (inscription and coin)

CHÂTEAUDUN: The State (Monuments Historiques)

CASA DE PILATOS: The Duke of Medinaceli and Alcala. *Phot. de Arte M. Moreno*, 39

VILLA LANTE: Dottore Angelo Cantoni. *Pucci Foto*, 46

SCHLOSS TRATZBERG: Graf Sighart Enzenberg. *Fot. Demanega*, 55

PALAZZO DEL TE: Comune di Mantova. *Soprintendenza alle Gallerie di Mantova*, 60, 62, 63

CHAMBORD: The State (Monuments Historiques). *Mansell Collection*, 70

VILLA D'ESTE: The State (Ministero della Pubblica Istruzione). *Victoria & Albert Museum, London*, 78

EGESKOV: Count Gregers Ahlefeld-Bille

VILLA MASER: Contessa Marina Luling Buschetti Volpi. *Mansell Collection*, 95

HARDWICK HALL: National Trust (The Duke of Devonshire). *Trustees of the Chatsworth Settlement*, 100 (accounts). *National Trust*, 100 (two portraits)

CAPRAROLA: The State. *Gabinetto delle Stampe, Milan*, 106. *Archives of Parma*, 109

HÔTEL LAMBERT: Baron Alexis de Redé

TANLAY: Marguerite de Tanlay, Comtesse de la Chauvinière. *Victoria & Albert Museum, London*, 120, 123

ISOLA BELLA: Prince Vitaliano Borromeo. *Gabinetto delle Stampe, Milan*, 131

VAUX-LE-VICOMTE: Madame Sommier. *Mansell Collection*, 136

WILTON: Earl of Pembroke and Montgomery. *Worcester College, Oxford*, 140

DROTTNINGHOLM: H. M. the King of Sweden. *Nordiska Museum*, 151. *Svenska Porträttarkivet Nationalmuseum, Stockholm*, 154

PALACIO DI LIRIA: Duke of Alba. *Hispanic Society of America*, 158

BLENHEIM PALACE: Duke of Marlborough. *British Museum*, 162, 166-7. *National Portrait Gallery*, 164 (three portraits)

475 HEERENGRACHT, AMSTERDAM: Hollandsche Societeit voor Levensverzekeringen. *Coll. Kon. Academie v. Wetenschappen*, 171, 172 (Philips). *Coll. Jhr. van Lennep*, 172 (two paintings). *Rijksdienst v/d Monumentenzorg*, 173

PALAIS SCHWARZENBERG: Prince Schwarzenberg. *Photo, Anton Fesl*, 181 (carpet)

PALAZZO LABIA: M. Charles de Beistegui

THE NYMPHENBURG: Land of Bavaria. From '*Nymphenburg*', by Luisa Hager, *Hirmer Verlag*, 190, 194, 195 (three portraits)

STUPINIGI: Ordine dei SS. Maurizio e Lazzaro. *Museo Civico, Turin*, 198, 200 (Juvara)

POMMERSFELDEN: Gräfin Schönborn. '*Pommersfelden*', by H. Kreisel, *Hirmer Verlag*, 207, 208 (plan and portrait), 211

BRÜHL: Stadt Köln. *Rheinisches Bildarchiv, Köln*, 214, 216

WÜRZBURG: Land of Bavaria. '*Die Fresken der Würzburger Residenz*', *Hirmer Verlag*, 221, 229. *Victoria & Albert Museum, London*, 224

CLAYDON: National Trust (Ralph Verney Esq.). *Sydney W. Newbury, phot.*, 232 (two portraits)

RUSSBOROUGH: Sir Alfred Beit. *National Library of Ireland*, 239. *National Gallery of Ireland*, 240

SANS SOUCI: Government of the D. D. R. (Ministerium für Kultur). *Sans Souci Archives*, 246. *British Museum*, 244

BENRATH: Landeshaupstadt Düsseldorf. *Giraudon*, (*Palais de l'Élysée*), 251. *Kunstmuseum, Düsseldorf*, 252 (Pigage), 255, 256. *Schloss Nymphenburg*, 252 (Theodore)

SYON: Duke of Northumberland. *The 'Connoisseur' and the Duke of Northumberland*, 262-3. *R. B. Fleming & Co. Ltd*, 261, 264

YOUSSOUPOFF: Leningrad Town Council. *Mansell Collection*, 270. *Prince Felix Youssoupoff*, 271

QUELUZ: The State of Portugal. *British Museum*, 277

PETIT TRIANON: Musée de Versailles. *Archives Nationales*, 282, 284. *Mansell Collection*, 288 (two portraits)

ARBURY: Humphrey Fitzroy Newdegate Esq. *P. W. & L. Thompson, phot. Coventry*, 292 (Deviss and Wren). *Phot. Logan, Birmingham*, 292 (Beighton)

HÔTEL D'HANE: Comte de Bousies-Borluut. *National Portrait Gallery*, 300 (Wellington)

LAZIENKI: City of Warsaw. *Muzeum Narodowe, Warsaw*, 304, 306. *Polska Akademia Nauk*, 308 (Cerberus), 309 (plan). *Edward Hartwig*, 306 (south and north fronts), 307 (all three pictures)

CASITA DEL LABRADOR: Patrimonio Nacional. *Patrimonio Nacional*, 313, 314. *Prado Museum*, 315